The Barefoot Retirement Plan

Safely Build a Tax-Free Retirement Income Using a Little-Known 150 Year Old Proven Method That Beats the Pants Off Other Plans

America's Most Powerful Retirement Plan

Now *YOU* Can Use the Same Wealth Creation Methods the Rich Use To Create Your Dream Retirement

DOYLE SHULER

Copyright Notice

This book and all related materials are copyrighted © 2014 by Barefoot Retirement. All rights reserved.

No part of this publication may be copied, changed in any format, sold, reproduced or transmitted in any form or by any means, electronic or mechanical, or used in any way other than what is outlined within this book under any circumstances.

ISBN-13: 978-1502482570
ISBN-10: 1502482576

Table of Contents

1. Dedication 5
2. Introduction 7
3. The Retirement Dream 9
4. Your FREE Retirement CheckUP 13
5. FREE Barefoot Retirement LIVE Webinar 17
6. The Retirement Crisis in America 18
7. Tired Of Being Whack-A-Mole 26
8. Paper Profits and Investment Fantasies 31
9. I Knew There Had To Be A Better Way 50
10. The Solution – The Barefoot Retirement Plan 54
11. Part 1: The Guaranteed Index Account 65
12. How It Works 79
13. S&P 500 vs IUL – Who Wins? 95
14. More Unbeatable Benefits 102
15. Creating A Lifetime Income 115
16. How Does the IUL Compare To a ROTH IRA 119
17. Part 2: Outside Investment Accelerator or (Double Dipping) 123
18. Maximizing The Barefoot Retirement Program ... 137

19. The Barefoot Retirement Calculator 147

20. Barefoot Business Owners Program 157

21. The Best College Savings Program You've Never Heard Of 169

22. Build a Retirement and Leave a Legacy 172

23. Frequently Asked Questions 176

24. What We Know and What We Don't Know 180

25. How To Get Started 184

26. Two Paths to Choose From 188

27. For Insurance Professionals 191

28. Your Free, No-Obligation Analysis Request Form 192

29. General Disclaimer 195

The Barefoot Retirement Plan

Special Notice

This book is not intended to give financial investment or tax advice of any kind nor is it intended to make or suggest any personal investment or tax recommendations about strategies that individuals should or should not choose. We are not investment advisors nor registered securities dealers. Everyone's situation is unique. While the strategies discussed in this book are working extremely well at the moment, no one can guarantee they will continue to work in the future. You should always seek the advice of qualified professionals who are very experienced in these exact areas of specialization and who thoroughly understands these strategies and concepts. The intent of this book is to educate and introduce unique and powerful strategies and concepts for retirement planning. The strategy also allows for a unique leveraging option if you seek to achieve higher overall returns through optional outside investments. Hopefully, the concepts revealed in this book will open your eyes to an entire new world of little-known and excellent retirement options that are available.

About This Book

I want to be crystal clear about this. This is not a generic book about retirement. It's a book that highlights the retirement crisis in America, and it offers a specific solution that we believe is the absolute finest retirement solution on the planet. *It's really that good*. And yes, probably about 99%+ of the people reading this book have never even heard of this solution before.

To be completely transparent, I am a partner in a company that offers and provides some of the solutions mentioned in this book. True, there are other sources available for the strategies and solutions mentioned in this book. We have yet to find another book in the marketplace that reveals the unique strategies and solutions that we offer. If it bothers you that we are writing about a solution we offer, then this book is probably not for you. If you are truly looking for the most perfect retirement solution ever created, *then you're going to love this book.*

To The Reader

If you're like most people and hate reading boring and complicated books about finance, then you're in for a treat. This book is intentionally written in a conversational style, and we go out of our way to avoid using fancy industry lingo that many lay people don't understand. Our goal is not to impress you with how smart we are, rather our goal is to help you to easily and clearly understand what could be one of the single most important aspects of your life, retirement. It's a very serious subject, but we've really tried to make it easy to understand, enlightening and as fun to read as possible. I think you'll enjoy this.

Disclaimer

A great deal of care, effort and attention has been taken to provide current and accurate information regarding the subject matter covered in this book. Neither the author, Doyle Shuler, nor the publisher is responsible for any errors or omissions, or for the results obtained from the use of the information in this book. The information contained in this book is intended to provide general information and does not constitute financial, legal or investment advice. Please see the full disclaimer at the end of the book.

Chapter 1

Dedication

This book is dedicated to all the hard working, tax-paying citizens of America, who are striving for a better life and a better retirement.

To the free thinkers who have the courage to question the traditional financial and retirement advice and the confidence to conduct their own research and make their own fact-based decisions.

To all the people who are tired of blindly following the herd and not finding the results they deserve.

After all, it was Albert Einstein who said, "Blind belief in authority is the greatest enemy of truth."

To people who seek the truth and seek a better way.

When you commit to becoming an independent thinker, you unleash the freedom within to boldly live your life on your own terms.

And to all who seek a barefoot retirement of their own.

You truly are my inspiration.

CHAPTER 2

Introduction

I remember an old story told by Zig Ziglar many years ago about the man who was walking along the road and found a chest of gold. The man went through many trials and challenges as a result of finding the gold. In the end, he discovered that simply keeping all the gold for himself, did not make him happy and fulfilled. In the end, he was only able to find true peace and happiness when he discovered that it was more important to share the gold with others whom you love and care about.

I'm sure many of you are like me in that, you've been through the school of hard knocks and real world university. Sure I've had some great financial wins and blessings, and I'm very grateful for them. However, I've also had more financial challenges and disappointments along the way than I care to remember. It's not often that you find anything that's so positive and potentially life-changing, as I have found with this program. As you will soon see, it really is that good!

My only regret is that I did not find this plan earlier in life. I can't change that but I can do all that I can to share this with as many others as I can. I know that by enriching other's lives, we enrich our own lives. That's why we are so motivated to share this.

I'm a proud, hardworking, tax-paying, God-fearing American, and it saddens me to see that there are so many people in this great country of ours who are so unprepared and underfunded for retirement. Most of them have simply followed the rules and tried to do exactly what the *"experts"* have told us to do to adequately prepare for retirement. In spite of all that *expert* advice, best efforts and intentions, the big majority of American's finances are not even close to where they need to be in order for them to have the kind of retirement that want.

My goal is to help as many people as possible to have the kind of retirement they desire and deserve. Hopefully, this book will open your eyes to what's really happening and give you some great ideas and action plans that will help you make wiser retirement decisions.

Enjoy this book. Feel free to share it with others whom you care about. I wish you the barefoot retirement of your dreams.

CHAPTER 3

The Retirement Dream

Ahhhh ... Retirement. The long-awaited time in our lives when we can finally slow down, kick back, relax, and enjoy the finer things in life. Spend that precious time with family and loved ones, travel and really start to experience and appreciate life the way we've always wanted to. What a magical time in our lives.

Unfortunately, a huge number of Americans are never going to get to experience the story-book retirement that we've always dreamed about. The harsh reality is, for many, it's going to be the most difficult and challenging time in their lives. However, it doesn't have to be that way.

Not at all.

I promise you within the pages of this book; you will discover the finest and most beneficial retirement plan you've ever seen. Really, it's that good.

If you were to force me to name one negative thing about this plan, I simply could not do it. When you factor in all the benefits this plan offers, and honestly compare them to anything else out there, you'll see for yourself that this really is *America's most powerful retirement plan!*

What I'm going to reveal to you is something that less than 1% of Americans know about. The ultra-rich have been using a similar strategy for decades, but the average investment advisor doesn't have a clue about it.

Seriously, this plan is downright amazing. It's so innovative that a patent has been placed on it. So far, it's only been available to a tiny percentage of people. However, it's no longer just for the super-rich. The Barefoot Retirement program is now available to almost anyone, as well as the rich. It's available to anyone who wants to have the retirement of their dreams.

While reading this book, your eyes will be opened to hope and new possibilities. A new way of life. The information contained within this book truly has the potential, if acted upon, to dramatically change your retirement for the better. *Much better!*

Here's the issue. Some people spend more time planning a vacation than they spend planning their retirement. How unfortunate. Think about this. Today the average person entering retirement has a life expectancy of 84 years. If you retire at 65, you'll spend 19 years of your life in retirement. That's about 23% of your entire life spent in retirement! Yikes. That's huge.

That's a very long time for your retirement funds to last and serve you. Plus, you know just how unstable the world and the economy has become. Who knows what types of unforeseen challenges we'll face in the coming decades that we can't even imagine right now? Retirement planning is very serious business, and it's critically important that you get this right.

We're on a mission.

The Barefoot Retirement team's mission is to help as many people as we can, salvage, turnaround, change, improve, and make-over their retirement program so it will be there to support and sustain them during those golden retirement years and enable them to have the barefoot retirement of their dreams.

What Does *"Barefoot Retirement"* Mean?

If you're asking yourself, *"What the heck, is a barefoot retirement?"* Let me explain. Barefoot Retirement is a metaphor for living the type of retirement you dream about. It's all about *FREEDOM*. Freedom to kick your shoes off, anytime you want, and live life on your own terms. Barefoot is simply a representation of having that freedom and independence. So if you're not a literal barefoot kind-of-person, that's perfectly fine. You can keep your shoes on, and still have the freedom to enjoy life on your own terms. More on this shortly.

Who Is This Book For?

- It's for anyone who's concerned that the current plan you're on is not going to get you where you want to be.
- It's for anyone who already has sufficient retirement funds in place, but wants to do better and wants to keep more of their hard-earned money during retirement.
- It's for anyone who is scared to death that tax rates are going to go to the moon and will rob you of the funds you need to sustain your retirement.
- It's for anyone who's been listening to the *"traditional"* financial advisors and taking the *"traditional"* financial advice, and is frustrated that your retirement fund seems stuck in the mud and going nowhere.
- It's for anyone who needs to make up lost ground quickly, but wants to make it up safely.
- It's for anyone who is open-minded to new ideas and is willing to do their own due diligence to determine what options are truly best for you and your family.

CHAPTER 4

Your FREE Retirement CheckUP

As promised, we want to give you a FREE Barefoot Retirement CheckUP. We had this CheckUP built exclusively for us, and it's the only one of its kind in the world.

We could easily charge $500 for these checkups. Some companies charge much more than that. But that's not what we're about. We want to give you your CheckUP completely and totally free!

Think about this. The average person will spend 25% to 30% of their life in retirement. **Doesn't it just make good sense to get a retirement checkup?**

If you're not on track to reach your retirement goals, wouldn't you want to know about it sooner than later? Trust me, you don't want to wait until shortly before you're due to retire, and then find out that you're off the mark and won't have the funds you need, for as long as you need them to last.

After all, we get checkups for our health. We get checkups for our cars. We get checkups for our teeth, our kids, our pets, our homes, our boats, and even our heating & air units. Just about anything that's really important to us, we get it checked up.

So when's the last time you had a retirement checkup?

If you're like most people, it's been quite a while, if ever. Here's the good news. **Our CheckUP is *fast* and easy.** You simply fill out an online form with about ten questions. If you pretty much know your information, you can complete the CheckUP in about 2-minutes. Your CheckUP results are emailed to you within 24 hours or less.

People love how SIMPLE our CheckUP results are. Many other checkup programs provide complicated and confusing results that leave you more confused. You will find our results to be crystal clear and extremely simple.

Your results will be clearly laid out in front of you in black & white. We even include charts & graphs to make it easy to understand. Your CheckUP will show you:

- How prepared you are now to reach your retirement goals
- If you stay on your current course, what your retirement picture will look like once you get there
- If and/or when your retirement funds will run out
- Variables you can control now, before you retire, that can give you a more secure and prosperous retirement

If you are NOT on track to reach your retirement goals, we will show you:

- How much more you need to be saving each year
- How much higher rate of return you need on your current funds
- How much longer you may need to work before you are able to retire
- How much you may need to reduce your spending during retirement

Plus if you're not on track to reach your retirement goals, we'll give you specific actions you can take NOW to insure you can reach them.

We sincerely hope that our Retirement CheckUP will help you to make wiser and more educated retirement planning decisions. It is our gift to you, completely free!

Just as many others have done, please feel free to share the CheckUP with your friends, family, loved ones, employees, or anyone you care about. Anyone can take the CheckUP. And it's completely free to everyone who takes it.

To Access Your Free Barefoot Retirement CheckUP Go To:

BarefootRetirement.com/CheckUP

Why worry about what your retirement will look like when you can find out for sure in just a few minutes? And, it won't cost you a cent.

Get yours today!

CHAPTER 5

FREE Barefoot Retirement LIVE Webinar

Periodically we host live webinars to help people get a better understanding of the Barefoot Retirement Program, and how it can revolutionize your retirement plans. We get lots of compliments on these webinars and most of our clients absolutely love them.

To view our upcoming schedule of live webinars, and reserve your seat at a time and date that's convenient for you, please go to:

BarefootRetirement.com/webinar

We look forward to seeing you on the next webinar.

CHAPTER 6

The Retirement Crisis in America

Our Government and the main street media don't want to talk about the retirement crises that's unfolding right before our eyes. They don't want to shine a spotlight of truth on the looming retirement train-wreck in America.

Why you ask? They don't want to scare everyone to death. Make no mistake about it. It's out there. If you listen quietly and pay attention, you'll hear it. It's coming. And coming fast. It's like an out-of-control freight train. And it's headed right for us. And if you don't prepare for it, it's going to slam right into you.

Forbes.com ran an article on 3-20-13 called **"The Greatest Retirement Crisis in American History."** The article stated, "We will witness millions of elderly Americans, the Baby Boomers and others, slipping into poverty. Too frail to work, too poor to retire, will become the 'new normal' for many elderly Americans."

The *average* 401(k) balance for 65 year olds is estimated at $25,000 by independent experts, (or $100,000 if you believe the retirement planning industry). Economics Professor Teresa Ghilarducci estimates that 75% of Americans nearing retirement in 2010 had less than $30,000 in their retirement accounts.

> The Forbes article when on to say: *"Americans also know the great 401k experiment of the past 30 years has been a disaster. It is now apparent that 401ks will **not** provide the retirement security promised to workers."*

Did you see the TIME Magazine cover, **"Why It's Time to Retire the 401(k)."** In the article it said;

> **"The ugly truth, though, is that the 401(k) is a lousy idea, a financial flop, a rotten repository for our retirement reserves."**

In this eye-opening article, they also spoke of what they thought was the solution. We agree with their recommended solution, but more on that in a bit.

I know this is some seriously scary stuff. Most Americans are vastly unprepared for retirement and for some, they're literally scared to death. In fact, check out this recent survey. It found that 61% of Americans FEAR running out of money when they retire **MORE** than they fear death itself! Wow. Is that a sobering statistic or what?

Respondents Age 44 to 75

The 60 Minutes Story About Retirement Being Broken In America.

60 Minutes ran an eye-popping story about what a huge disappointment 401(k)s have been and how they have failed so many Americans.

I encourage you to take a few minutes and what this shocking 60 Minutes story. You can view it by going to: www.BarefootRetirement.com/60minutes

A massive 28% of the American population are baby boomers. Some reached retirement age a few years ago. Now 10,000 baby boomers are retiring every single and every day. Even so, the vast majority of boomers are not yet there. There are 88 million more boomers on the way. That's a good thing because most of them are nowhere near ready for retirement.

Heck, over half of all Baby Boomers are still supporting their adult children. Others are supporting their elderly parents. How are they supposed to adequately save for their retirement when they're still supporting others and trying to survive themselves?

Make no mistake about it. There IS a retirement crises in America. As it plays out over the next few decades, people are going to be shocked at how dramatically this is going to change our way of life.

Here's another survey by Gallup that shows you how the fear of running out of money during retirement stacks up against the other fears out there:

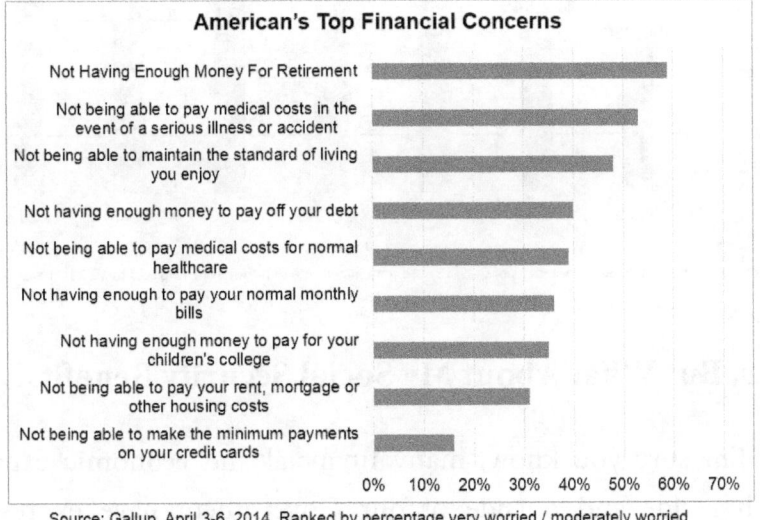

Source: Gallup, April 3-6, 2014 Ranked by percentage very worried / moderately worried

Maintaining Your Purchasing Power During Retirement

Another challenge we all face is inflation. Too many people don't stop and seriously consider the longer-term effects of inflation. Especially if you're on a fixed income. **Since 1925, inflation has averaged 3% a year.** (Source: Global Financial Data, Inc.)

As you can see in the chart below, if you had an income of $50,000 per year in 2013, you would need to have an income of $89,596 to maintain the same purchasing power just 20 years later. When planning your needs during retirement, be sure to factor in inflation.

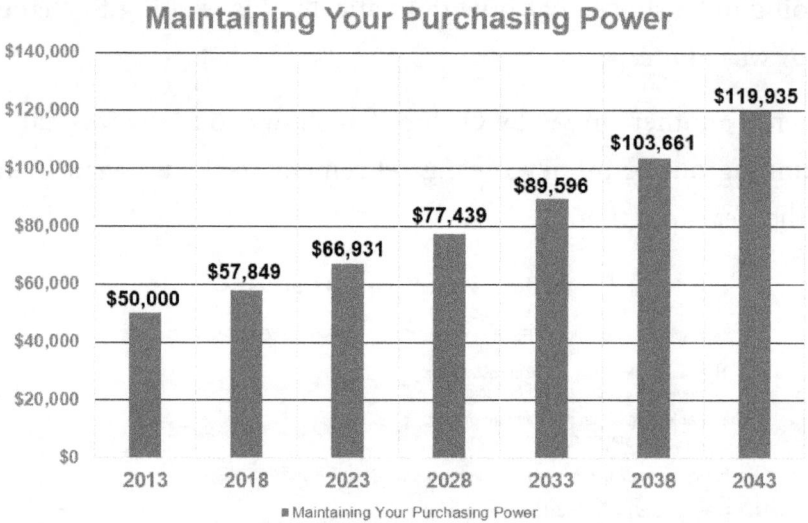

Source: Global Financial Data, Inc. as of 5-22-12, CPI annualized rate of return from 12-31-25 to 12-31-11 was 3.0%

Yes, But What About My Social Security Benefits?

As I'm sure you know, many financial and economic experts both inside and outside of our Government have expressed doubt about the Social Security program and its ability to survive long term. If you are counting on Social Security as one of your main sources of retirement funds, it may be wise to seek some other options just in case these experts are right.

In fact, most people never even notice this, but this is the exact statement you will find on the very first page of your 2014 Social Security statement:

> **About Social Security's future…**
>
> Social Security is a compact between generations. Since 1935, America has kept the promise of security for its workers and their families. Now, however, the Social Security system is facing serious financial problems, and action is needed soon to make sure the system will be sound when today's younger workers are ready for retirement.
>
> Without changes, in 2033 the Social Security Trust Fund will be able to pay only about 77 cents for each dollar of scheduled benefits.* We need to resolve these issues soon to make sure Social Security continues to provide a foundation of protection for future generations.

Two points on this. First, if this is what the actual agency is saying about their own financial health, it leads one to wonder just how accurate this is. The Government seems to be handing out the *"Free Government Cheese"* as fast as they possibly can, to everyone they can, regardless if they are legal US citizens or not. So at the rate they are burning through all of that Government money, it makes you wonder how long the Social Security Trust Fund will really last.

Second, it stinks that the Government promised you this benefit and will, in all likelihood, not be able to come through with it. You have done what was required of you and paid a lot of money into the Social Security system. You upheld your end of the bargain. Now you get the short end of the stick. This is especially bad for younger people. They will have to continue paying their full amount into the system knowing full well that they may not receive anything back in return for it. So if you are relying on Social Security for your "Retirement Program," you may want to take matters into your own hands and develop a Plan-B, just in case.

Yes, But What About My Pension Plan?

You've probably heard about all the pension fund problems there are with Government pensions as well as some corporate pension programs. Hopefully, they will survive and thrive but their future is looking dim.

Pension plans are similar to Social Security in that they are nothing more than promises that can be broken.

During the years from 1996 through 2007, 25% of all the Fortune 500 company pension plans have been terminated, closed or frozen. That's a staggering number.

In a study conducted by Hewitt Consulting (now Aon Hewitt) it was found that if the same rate of decline in pension funds that occurred from 2002 through 2008 continues, (something the company considers unlikely), there will be no more open-plan pension funds in the Fortune 500 by the year 2019.

I sat beside a guy on a flight years ago, who was one of the top Federal officials in charge of the Federal Pension Benefit Guarantee Corporation (PBGC).

A lot of people feel a great sense of security knowing that the PBGC is there to back them up in case their employer's pension fund goes belly up. I remember how shocked I was when this fellow told me about the tiny fraction of pensions that they could bail out if there were large numbers of pension failures. It would be like trying to bail out the ocean with a thimble. If the problem is small, they can handle it. If it becomes widespread, you had better have another plan.

Can You Relate To This?

Most middle and upper-middle-class Americans are pretty much in the same boat and have been down the same pathway. We've been faithfully following the rules and doing what all of the *"experts"* have been telling us.

Things like: *"Contribute to your IRA, invest in your company 401(k), invest in solid mutual funds, stay the course, buy and hold, hang in there, keep the faith, just keep on investing and over time, the stock market will deliver the best return, and you'll be able to retire comfortably and enjoy your retirement years the way you deserve to."*

I've got a question for you.
How's all that *"expert"* financial advice working out for you so far?

CHAPTER 7

Tired Of Being Whack-A-Mole

Remember back in the year 2000 and what good times those were? Dot.com stocks were flying high. Equities were breaking all-time records every day. It seemed like there was nothing but blue skies and prosperity ahead for all of us. Then the unexpected happened.

BAM... Many of us lost 50% or more of our retirement savings in the dot.com bust. The NASDAQ technology stocks plunged 78% from March 10, 2000 to October 9th, 2002. It was ugly! It's interesting to note that even more than a decade later, the NASDAQ is <u>STILL</u> below its highpoint in 2000.

For the smarter people who did not get so caught up in the Dot.com stocks, the S&P 500 got caught in the market downdraft and lost 49% during that same 2½ year time period. When all of the dust settled from the Dot.com crash, over 9.5 Trillion of American's wealth had disappeared! Along with the wealth that disappeared, many people's retirement dreams also disappeared with the crash.

Then, just as we were beginning to recover from the Dot.com carnage and finally start gaining some positive ground with our retirement accounts, **BAM**… We got hit with the 2008/2009 stock market crash and many lost another 40% or 50% of their retirement account values. The S&P 500 lost 57% from its high point in October of 2007 through March of 2009. It was not a happy time at all.

It used to be that we always knew we had our home-equity value to fall back on. After all, many of us had been faithfully paying our home mortgages for decades because we knew that our home would always grow in value and our home would eventually be an important part of our retirement program.

Everything was going great, right up until the 2007 housing crisis hit and then **BAM**… Many of our home values dropped like a rock. I knew some people whose home values dropped by more than 50%. I think all of us have friends and loved ones, (and possibly even ourselves), who ended up losing their homes, short selling them or having them foreclosed. Talk about adding insult to injury, this was a hard blow to stomach for all of us.

The 2008/2009 market crash and the housing bust caused another 14.8 Trillion of American wealth to disappear!

Remember the old *Whack-A-Mole* arcade game? It's the one where you hold a mallet and every time a mole pops his head up, **BAM...** you whack it back down. And you keep whacking them and whacking them, every time they poke their little heads up.

Are you feeling like that Whack-A-Mole? Every time you finally start to get ahead... and just when you begin to start looking forward to opening your investment account statements again...**BAM**, it seems like something else always comes along and whacks us down again.

A Friend's Story

I vividly remember the 2008/2009 stock market crash. A close friend of mine at that time was a senior-level investment manager at one of the largest and commonly known investment firms in America. He had been with that company for over 35 years. This guy was *"in the know."* He had all of the real-time and cutting-edge market information anyone could ever hope to get. We would often go to dinner and play golf together. He constantly told me how strong the market was and how promising our investment future was. Things were just going up and up, and the future was brighter than ever!

Sadly, his health started to decline. He only had two more years before he planned to retire. He decided to hang in there and stick it out until retirement. I remember him telling me this like it was yesterday. I called him shortly after the stock market crashed. When most of the dust had settled, he had lost about 65% of everything he had worked his entire life to acquire.

Here's the lesson from this that hit me like a ton of bricks.

This guy did investing for a living. He was an experienced 35 year industry veteran. While I was busy traveling and working in my business, I had always envied that he had the luxury of time to watch the markets 24/7. He had the finest corporate market data at his fingertips, from one of the largest financial institutions in the world. If anybody should have seen the crash coming and prepared for it, he should have. He didn't. He did not have one clue about it, right up until the end. It caught him and countless others completely by surprise.

I only lost somewhere in the high 40% range of my investment portfolio in that crash. The expert with all the best information in the world, and doing this professionally, (not an amateur like me), lost 65%. I spent many sleepless nights thinking about this. It was a hopeless feeling. I kept saying to myself *"How do I, as an amateur investor, stand a chance if an expert like this, got creamed?"* It's like a rigged game, and we're the pawns in the game, that get sacrificed.

My friend was 2 years away from retirement, and he lost 65% of everything he had! Plus, he was in poor health. He was devastated. I remember saying to myself that I wanted to do everything I could to avoid ever being in a situation like that, and particularly when I was so close to retirement.

CHAPTER 8

Paper Profits and Investment Fantasies

I Got Sick and Tired of Being Sick and Tired.

I got tired of being whacked down every time I started getting ahead. I was feeling like I was a little pawn in a giant chess game. The big guys were just using all of us in their economic games. I finally had enough. Plus, I was running out of time. After all, how many 40% to 50% hits can you take to your life savings and still be able to retire as you had planned?

Did you know that it takes a 100% gain to recover from a 50% loss? It's true. Also, a 50% loss will wipe out a 100% gain. How long do you think it takes most people to recover from a 50% loss? As I am writing this (Summer of 2014), it has taken from July of 2009, until now, for the DJIA (Dow Jones Industrial Average) to climb back up approximately 100% to where it was in July of 2009. That's almost 5 years, and that was during a good stock market time period. And that's just to break even and be in the same place you were about 5 years ago.

Plus, you can never get those years back nor their lost earning potential. My investment friend who lost 65% would have only recently gotten back to where he was almost 6 years ago if he stayed in the markets. Who wants to delay retirement plans that long? Playing catch up all the time just plain stinks.

What About Inflation?

Yep, let's not forget about our old friend inflation. If you go to:

www.usinflationcalculator.com you can see that we've had over 10% inflation since 2009.

Plus, we've had a whopping 37.2% inflation since the year 2000. That takes a huge bite out of your dollars' purchasing power!

> If we look at the total return of the S&P 500 since 2000, the real... inflation-adjusted purchasing power of your investments is STILL LESS than it was 14 years ago. *(Gee, wonder why your stockbroker doesn't tell you that?)*

Nothing Goes Up Forever

When you're planning your retirement, timing is everything. Take a look at the chart below. We know for sure that every so often, the financial markets crash. They then take years to recover. If you're young, time is on your side. If you're nearing retirement, a loss such as the ones shown below can be devastating, and can turn your retirement dreams into a nightmare, overnight.

Time Period	Percentage of Stock Market Loss	Years To Recover
1901-1903	46%	2 Years
1906-1907	49%	9 Years
1916-1917	40%	2 Years
1919-1921	47%	3 Years
1929-1932	89%	22 Years
1939-1942	40%	3 Years
1973-1974	45%	8 Years
1987-1987	36%	3 Years
2000-2003	32%	6 Years
2007-2008	49%	5 Years
When Will The Next One Happen?	How Big Will The Loss Be?	How Long Will It Take To Recover?

Based on the market data above, the market loses 47% every 11 years!

Losing money stinks!

Losing 47% every 11 years, is downright stupid.

And, these kinds of losses will keep you from having the retirement you want and deserve.

The best single thing we can all do to preserve our wealth and, best prepare for retirement is to faithfully follow Warren Buffett's #1 rule for investing success.

Warren Buffett's Rules Form Investing
Rule #1: Never Lose Money
Rule #2: Never Forget Rule #1

Seriously, if you're trying to plan for something as serious as your retirement in an environment like this, how can you succeed?

The truth is, you can't.

If you're an average person playing by the mainstream rules that Wall Street, and the major investment firms are encouraging you to play by, you won't win, and you can't win.

Doesn't The *"Smart Money"* Invest Their Money in the S&P 500?

This is often true. Many wise investors know, according to the Standard & Poor's, over 99% of mutual funds consistently underperform the S&P 500 Index. That's why a lot of smart investors put their funds into something like a Vanguard S&P 500 Index Fund. It has a low expense ratio, and simply follows the S&P 500 index, which outperforms 99% of the managed mutual funds.

How *SAFE* are you feeling about being in the markets now?

Take a look at the chart below. It shows the performance of the S&P 500 from the year 2000, up until summer of 2014. Around the year 2000, the S&P 500 began a decline which ended in a 48% drop. Around 2008, the index began a decline which ended in a 56% drop. (Some people call these drops, *retirement killers*.) Take a look at where it is now. It certainty looks like the S&P 500 could begin another huge drop, at any time now. Don't you think?

Here's the problem. People have been saying the same thing every day, since 2011. Since that time, a lot of *"experts"* have been telling people to get out of the market *NOW*, before it falls off a cliff again. Had you taken their advice, and gotten out back then, you would have missed a huge up-side gain. Most of us are the same. We don't want to miss the up-side gains, but we are also scared to death, that it's going to crash again, and we will lose another 50% of our portfolio. Who can afford to go through that again?

I'm here to tell you there is a better way. A *MUCH* better way. The Barefoot Retirement Plan allows to you participate in most of the up-side gains… and TOTALLY eliminates any and all losses due to market declines. With our program, you don't have to watch the financial channels 24/7, and worry about when the next crash will really happen. You just relax and live your life. If the markets go up, your account will go up. If the markets crash, you are completely safe due to market downturns.

Caution. Please don't wait too long to get your Barefoot Retirement Plan set up, and in place! You don't have to be a financial guru to look at the chart below, and tell we're way overdue for another big correction, and/or crash.

Jeremy Grantham, co-founder and chief investment strategist of GMO, a Boston-based firm with $117 billion in assets under management, was recently quoted as saying, *"Another horrific stock market crash is coming, and the next bust will be "unlike* any other" we have seen. We have never had this before. It's going to be very painful for investors."

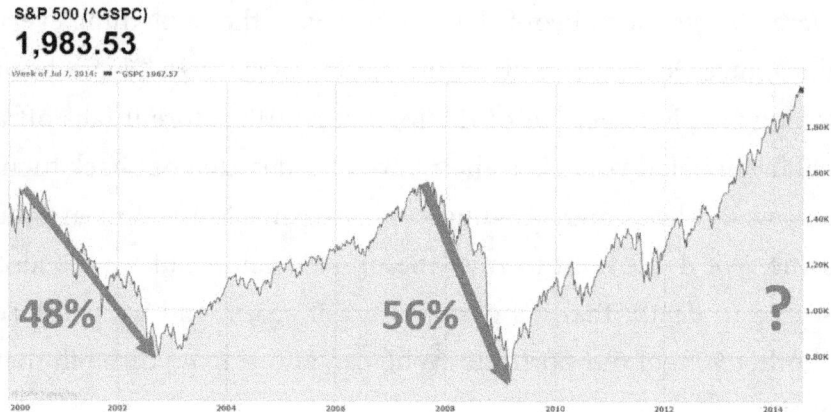

You can choose not to participate in the next big crash.

When you finish reading this book, you'll have more information than about 99% of other Americans have, on how to protect yourself, your family and your retirement. Don't wait until it's too late. Give us a call today, and let's take the first step to getting you protected.

"If I had to give advice, it would be keep out of Wall Street"

John D. Rockefeller

Let's Take a Look at the Returns AVERAGE Investors Are Earning

According to Dalbar, Inc., the nation's leading financial services market research firm, **over the last 20 years the average equity mutual fund investor has only earned 4.25% per year.** (Asset allocation funds and fixed-income funds performed dramatically worse over this same time period.) That is less than half the return that the S&P 500 returned over the same time period. **Plus, that 4.25% return only beats inflation by a puny 1.28% a year.**

Morningstar conducted a similar study, and the results were even worse. A 12.01% mutual fund return over 6 years, resulted into an **actual return of just 2.2% for investors.**

> When you think of all the stock market stress you've had over the last 20 years. The sleepless nights, the worry about the market, the calls to your broker, the roller-coaster price swings, and the anxiety of it all... to only come out 1.28% ahead of the game after playing by their rules for 20 years, *it's an insult really.*

If you find this interesting, I found a great little website, I think you will like. You simply enter any date range you want, and it will show you the AVERAGE returns versus the ACTUAL returns of the S&P 500. Plus, if you check the little box that says, "Adjust for Inflation," it will make you want to cry. Most of us don't want to really think about our actual returns because it makes us feel like a looser. Like a failure. If you want to build wealth, you just can't do it with the puny actual returns that average investors achieve. To check out the site, go to: moneychimp.com/features/market_cagr.htm

What About All of Those Investment Fees?

Let's not forget about all the fees that are charged by the various mutual funds and financial institutions. Some financial analyst estimate that over 90% of all financial advisers and planners can't even beat the S&P 500. In spite of that, you still get to pay all the relentless fees they charge for such poor performance.

Most people don't even realize this is going on. Forbes.com featured an article by Ty A. Bernicke, CFP where he did an in-depth analysis of mutual fund fees. The article was titled: **The Real Costs of Owning a Mutual Fund.** His findings are summarized below, and I think they speak for themselves.

Average Mutual Fund Cost Summary

Below is a summary of quantifiable costs and fees of the average mutual fund. The advisor costs and soft dollar costs are not included below due to the wide range in advisory fees and the difficulty of quantifying the soft dollar costs. If you work with a financial advisor, it is most important to add the advisory fees to the costs listed below to get an accurate view of your total potential costs.

Non-Taxable Account	Taxable Account
Expense Ratio .90%	Expense Ratio .90%
Transaction Costs 1.44%	Transaction Costs 1.44%
Cash Drag .83%	Cash Drag .83%
N/A	Tax Cost 1.00%
Total Costs **3.17%**	Total Costs **4.17%**

Over your life time, fees like this can absolutely kill your retirement. When you look at the average real returns investors are earning and the fees that are charged, it's enough to make you sick.

Demos, a public policy organization recently estimated that over a lifetime, a median-income two-earner family will pay nearly $155,000 in 401(k), and **IRA fees. This amount consumes**

nearly 1/3 of their ENTIRE investment returns. Higher-income dual-earner families pay as much as $277,969 in these types of fees. No wonder if feels like the deck is stacked against you.

Here are some startling facts recently presented in the PBS Frontline documentary, *"The Retirement Gamble."*

- 50% of Americans can't afford to save money for retirement
- 1/3rd have ZERO saved!
- 63% of your wealth is eaten up in fees over 5 decades.
- Average family will pay $155,000 in FEES to a 401k plan.
- 79% of mutual funds don't even beat the S&P 500.

John Bogle is the founder of Vanguard, the largest mutual fund company in the world. He is on record for saying, *"Fund investors do not earn the full market return… because fund investors incur costs, and costs are subtracted directly from the gross returns funds earn."* Bogle also said this about the 1990s bull market, *"The 6.5% annual return earned by fund investors was 3.3% behind the 9.8% annual return reported by the funds themselves."* Funny that they don't advertise the fact that investors made 1/3 less than what the funds show as their earnings.

Heck, just last month CBS 60 Minutes featured a story titled: **Is Wall Street a Rigged Game?** Michael Lewis thinks so. In the financial writer's new book titled Flash Boys, he blasts the so-called high-frequency traders he says are gaming the market. It's always the same-old story. The big guys win and screw over the little guys.

The story revealed how the big banks, stock exchanges and high-frequency traders have spent billions to game the system by using a technique called front running. They have sophisticated systems in place that can sniff out slower trades, jump in front of them, and make additional profits on the trades you are placing. These systems insure they win on every trade. These front running trades happen 100 times faster than the blink of an eye. Believe it or not, this is all perfectly legal. They went on to say that human beings have now been completely removed from the market place.

Wall Street is starting to look more like professional wrestling these days. You know it's fake. You know it's rigged, but some are still drawn to it. How can any average person, with average intelligence, and average information win in a rigged game like this? The truth is, they can't. Many of my friends now call this rigged stock market, **The Wall Street Casino**, and I agree with them.

Low Interest Rate Trap

Even though we are currently in one of the longest and strongest bull markets in history, US stock ownership is at a record low. Although less than half of Americans trust banks and financial services, many are forced to turn to fixed income options. Due to the government's low interest rate policy, fixed investments like money markets, CDs, etc. that used to pay solid guaranteed returns, NOW only pay a tiny 1% to 2% or so in returns.

Everyone knows itty-bitty returns like this, just won't cut it, and they certainly won't help you reach your retirement goals. Plus, after you factor inflation into the mix, you're really going backwards. And if you're just fed up with it all and decide to leave your money in a bank savings account, they're currently only averaging 0.06% interest, according to CNN Money. Over the last 24 years, our program has produced an average annual return of 9.28%. That means **our program has produced 154 times more than the banks are now paying you!**

Money Jail

If you choose to put your funds into a qualified plan like an IRA, or a 401(k), you are voluntarily choosing to subject yourself to an unending amount of restrictions, limitations, penalties, and requirements. They offer you the *"cheese,"* in the form of being able to put before taxed dollars into your retirement accounts. After you take the cheese, the door slams shut, and you are then locked in to all the requirements and restrictions imposed by these programs.

After all, have you actually read all the rules, regulations, requirements, restrictions, and legalese about these programs? They are similar to the tax code, in that they just go on, and on, and on, with a seemingly unending amount of rules, regulations and restrictions.

Putting your money into traditional qualified plans is somewhat like voluntarily locking your money up in money jail. Once they are locked up, they are then subject to these rules. You lose a good deal of your freedom-to-choose, and to make your own financial moves, based on your individual and unique needs. When you choose to put your money into these qualified plans, you are basically putting the Government in charge of your retirement.

When you voluntarily lock up your money in the usual qualified plans, you are subjecting them to a great deal of limitations and restrictions such as:

- **Limited contribution amounts**
- **Limited investment options**
- **Early withdrawal penalties**
- **Limited, to no loan options**
- **Forced distributions**

When you choose to put your funds into the Barefoot Retirement Plan, you are basically giving your money, and your access to it, **FREEDOM**. As you will discover shortly, our plan offers:

- **Unlimited contribution amounts**
- **Unlimited investment options**
- **No early withdrawal penalties**
- **Unlimited loan options**
- **No forced distributions**

We will show you how to *"legally"* break your money out of money jail, and give your money, and yourself, the freedom you deserve! Our program, gives the control to YOU.

Good News/Bad News… Retirees Are Living Longer

The average life expectancy for someone entering retirement today is currently 84 years of age. This age is just an average.

Over half will live beyond that — some will live into their 90s and even into their 100s. In fact, the Social Security Administration states that 25% of people turning 65 today will live past 90 years old and one out of 10 will live past 95.

While living longer is a wonderful thing and much better than the alternative, it's also causing retirees to try to figure out creative ways to make their retirement savings last an extra 10, 15, and 20 years. That's a tall order, especially at a time when health care costs are rising so rapidly. Even if you have the health and desire to work, jobs for the elderly are very scarce indeed.

My Sarasota Story

A few years ago, I was in Sarasota, Florida having lunch with clients. Sarasota is a big retirement area, and it's packed with retirees. It's a beautiful area. Lots of sun, gorgeous beaches, great restaurants, and a slower pace of life.

During lunch, we were talking about life in Sarasota, and one of my clients said, **"Yep, many of them retire at 65, and go back to work at 80."** It was one of those phrases that didn't register in my mind when I heard it, until a few moments later, so I said, "Wait, hang on a moment… and say that again please."

They said it was a pretty big thing there. Many people retire at 60 to 65 and move to Sarasota to soak up the sun and enjoy retired life. However, when some of them get around 80 years old, they find themselves running out of money. Sadly, many of them have no other options, so they have to try to find a job just to survive. Yikes! I had just never thought about that before, but it really weighed heavily on my mind. It used to be that when you retired, you stayed retired. Now, it's not necessarily the case.

Let me just say I totally understand the people who *"want"* to continue working as they get up in age because they love it. It keeps them sharp and gives them purpose. I get that. However, I can't imagine that represents a large percentage of retirees. I bet most of them have worked their guts out their entire life, and cherish the time to finally stop working, slow down, and enjoy doing the things *"they"* want to do.

Can you imagine how sobering it would feel to be 80 years old and wake up one morning and discover you have to go back to work? Heck, they probably haven't worked a job in 15 years. Their work skills are probably not exactly up to par, so it can't be easy to even find a job that anyone would want to do at that age.

I'm a ways from retirement myself, but I know how I feel some mornings waking up and having to get my body moving. I simply can't imagine how it must feel to be 80+ years old and have to wake up early every day, to go to a job that you don't want to do, but have to do, just to survive every day. Plus you'll likely be bossed around by a boss, who's a fraction of your age.

17% of retirees believe they retired too early, and should have kept working longer. I can't imagine this scenario is the vision that very many people have for retirement. But what are you going to do? If you run out of money, you've got to do something. That's why we're on a mission to help as many people as we can, properly set up a Barefoot Retirement Plan, so they will be able to make choices during their retirement and won't be forced to go back to work if they don't want to.

Higher Taxes and Cost of Living – Get Ready!

When making your retirement plans it's critical to factor in what your taxes will be, as well as cost of living increases. Some advisors will tell you that your taxes will go down in retirement because you'll be earning less money. This is not necessarily true and the time to figure this out is when there's still time to do something about it.

If your home is paid off you'll lose your mortgage interest deduction. If your kids have finally moved out on their own or aged out, you can no longer claim them as dependents, so you'll lose that deduction. There are a host of similar factors to consider but by far the biggest one, that's staring all of us square in the face, that most people don't what to talk about, is the overwhelming indebtedness of America. Let's see…

Our national debt is over 17 Trillion Dollars and rising fast

47 million Americans are on food stamps and climbing

Obama Care costs likely to skyrocket out of control

Entitlement programs soaring like never before

49% of Americans (voters) currently receive Government benefits

Fed is producing 85 billion of new money every month

Social Security, Medicare & Medicaid going broke

Plus, as many as 1/3 of the largest cities in American are facing possible bankruptcy.

I hate to be Mr. Gloom & Doom here, but this stuff is a really big deal! Someone has got to pay for all of this. Even if the Government were to tax all the super-rich fat cats at a 100% tax-rate, that won't even put a dent in it. The only way they're going to be able to pay for all of this is to raise our taxes. Desperate times call for desperate actions, and you can't ignore the transformation that's happening right in front of us.

We're in uncharted waters. No country in the world has experienced debt of this magnitude before. We have the largest government in the history of the world, and they are manipulating the largest economy in the world, and twisting the global market in ways that have never been done before. At some point, something has got to give, and when it does, *watch out*. Uncle Sam will be forced to raise taxes just to keep the Government Ponzi scheme going.

Take a look at the chart below. It was created by using the CBO (Congressional Budget Office) expenditure estimates. Looking at this chart, do you really see any way that taxes will EVER be able to go down in our lifetime? *Hardly!*

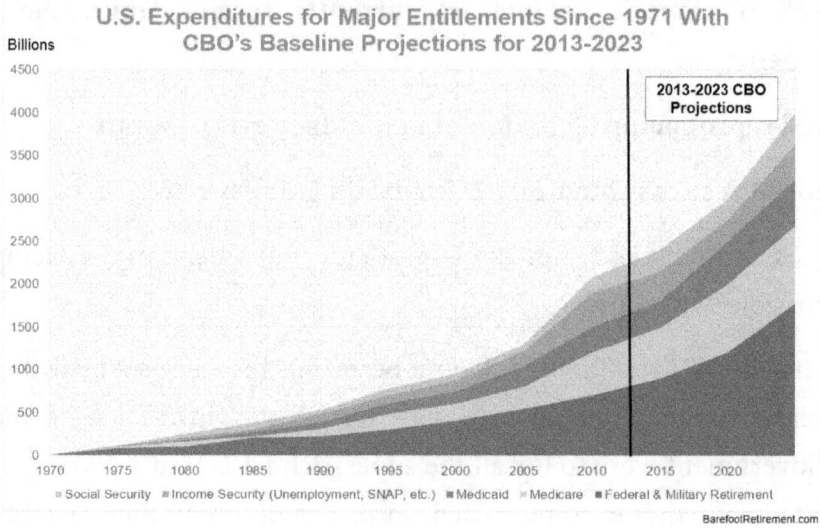

How High Can Tax Rates Go?

Obviously, no one knows just how high tax rates will go in the future, but we do know a few things. We know that history usually repeats itself. We also know that most people have very short memories.

Can you believe that the top Federal Marginal Tax Rates in the 1950s and part of the 1960s was **91%**? Could rates ever get that high again? That's up to you to answer for yourself.

It seems pretty obvious to me that if our Federal debt is at an all-time high and considering all the other economic challenges we are burdened with, at some point the Government will be forced to consider ALL options. If/when they can look back and say, *"We've done it before…."* Do you really think they won't think of this? The past history of rates being that high could give them precedence they need to do it again.

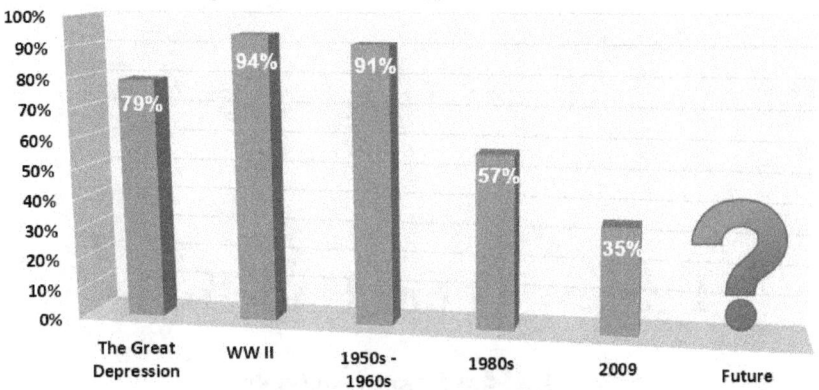

CHAPTER 9

I Knew There Had To Be A Better Way

I've always been an optimist. In spite of all this bad news, bad things that have happened, bad trends and negative forces out there, I just knew there had to be a better way to prepare for retirement. There had to be something out there that would work far better than the program I was on.

Here are some of the things I did know:

- I knew I wasn't getting any younger.
- I knew retirement was inevitability getting closer and closer.
- I knew retirement was coming, whether I was ready for it or not.
- I knew I did not want to be a Walmart greeter when I retired. ☺
- I knew what I had been doing was not working so great.

- I knew if I expected to get different results, I would need to do things differently.

- I knew that the main-stream financial industry was rigged, and that I would never win playing their rigged game.

- I knew I didn't want to risk participating in any more massive market crashes.

- I knew the rich had it figured out. They just keep getting richer and richer, regardless of the market swings and changes.

- I knew if I was going to find the answer, I was going to have to find out what the rich were doing differently and see if there was a way for me to (on a smaller scale) do what they were doing.

- I knew I was going to have to *"make up some lost financial ground"* to get my retirement account back to where I wanted it to be. Plus I needed to do it in a way that did not involve big risk. This meant I would have to find a way to safely get much higher returns on my investments and turn my money faster while limiting my downside.

- I knew if I looked long enough and hard enough, I could find the answer… *So I kept looking.*

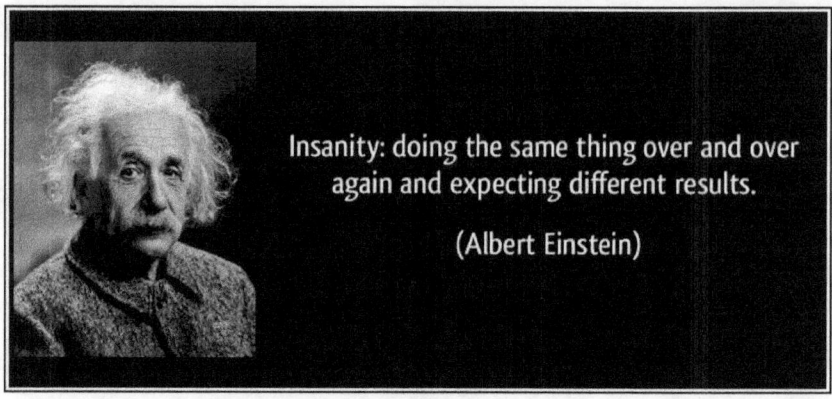

To make up the financial ground that I had lost, I knew I was going to have to focus on the velocity of my money. If I kept getting really small annual returns on my money, I knew I would not reach my retirement goals in time, and that wasn't an option.

It was kind of like being in the third quarter of a football game and being down by 28 points. I couldn't keep using running plays that would only gain a few yards at a time because that wouldn't win the game for me. The clock would run out on me if I chose that strategy. I needed to score some points pretty quickly if I wanted a chance to actually win the game before the clock ran out. And, I wanted to find a way to do it safely as well.

> **velocity of money**
> **noun** Economics.
> The frequency with <u>which</u> a single unit of currency or the total money supply turns over within the economy in a given year.

Talk about a tall order. I needed to grow my retirement account much faster than I've managed to do over the last few decades, and I needed to grow it safer than I had managed to in the past. I didn't have time to make any more mistakes or face any more setbacks. I needed to get it right.

I knew what I wanted my retirement to look like. And I definitely knew what I *DID NOT* want my retirement to look like. I just had not yet found a reliable plan to get me there. I knew it had to be out there somewhere. I just needed to find it, and find it pretty darn *fast!*

Everyone is going to retire at some point.

The Question Is...
What Will YOUR Retirement Look Like?

Which View Will You Have At Retirement?

Chapter 10

The Solution – The Barefoot Retirement Plan

The reason we call this The Barefoot Retirement Plan is because it represents FREEDOM. Freedom to CHOOSE to do what YOU want to do, when YOU want to do it. Freedom to kick your shoes off and relax if you wish.

After a lifetime of hard work, who wants to be forced to do things you don't want to do, because you have to do them? Barefoot symbolizes your retirement freedom and that's what we're all about. Helping you to structure your retirement so you'll have complete freedom when you retire to do whatever your heart desires.

Perhaps your dream is to walk barefoot on the beaches of the world. Or perhaps it's just to slow down and do all of those things you never had the time, energy or money to do while you had your nose to the grindstone, working hard every day, getting it done. Perhaps your dream is to walk barefoot in the park with your grand kids and feel like a kid again.

You know that *Ahhhh* feeling you have when you get home from a long day at work... and finally get a chance to kick your shoes off and wiggle your toes? *Ahhh*, it feels so good. That's the kind of feeling the Barefoot Retirement Plan can give you.

If your retirement is structured properly, you CAN have the freedom and peace of mind to enjoy your own barefoot retirement anyway you wish. We'd love to help you structure your barefoot retirement so you'll be able to kick your shoes off, wiggle your toes in the sand or the grass, take a deep breath, smile and live your life on your own terms.

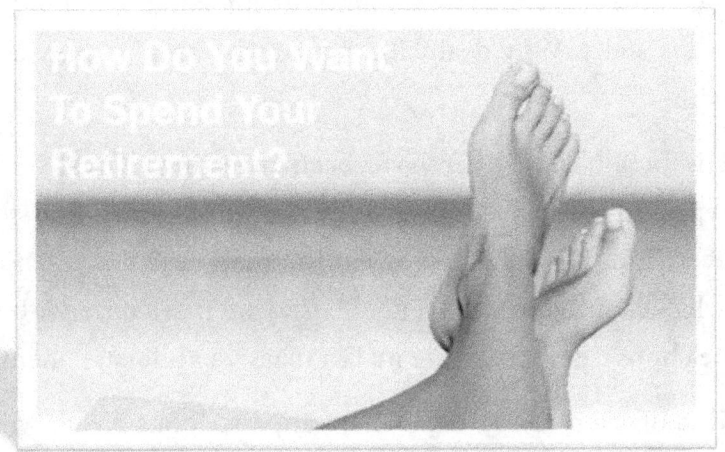

Let's continue...

I was in the process of developing an investment plan with one of the most successful investors in America. This guy developed his own system and an investment model flat out works. Over the past 19 years and after participating in over 900 million dollars' worth of transactions, he has NEVER had a losing deal. Amazing.

This guy is VERY private and only works with a private inner circle of investors. To date, he has had a little over 700 investor participants in his deals. Get this. He has a 98% repeat participation with his investors. Yep. Some retire and ride off into the sunset. But as soon as one deal is cashed out, 98% of his investors line up to reinvest in his next deal.

He maintains a small, private group of investors, and it's strictly *"by invitation only."* You have to be invited to participate. Outsiders can't just walk up and participate. Plus, he maintains a strict *"no hassles"* policy. If you give him any grief, and become a pain to deal with, you're out. Out for good. His philosophy is, life is short. Why deal with people who aren't a pleasure to deal with?

His bread and butter have been investing in real estate of all types. However, he is one of the most disciplined investors you'll ever find. He only buys when the market is down, and he only sells when the market is hot. To say he is selective with the deals he chooses to participate in, is a massive understatement.

Out of every 1,000 deals his company looks at, he will usually only find 1 or 2 that meet his strict requirements. That's why he doesn't lose. So when he can't find real estate deals that meet his strict criteria, he simply sits on the real estate sidelines and waits for the right market conditions before he gets back in.

While he is waiting for the right real-estate timing, he often invests in super-high quality debt deals. There's always a market somewhere, and he only does deals that he knows will work.

He is very shy when it comes to talking about this, but he has former Presidents, who are close personal friends. He's been on

Air Force One numerous times and even served on a HUD task force for former President George Bush Senior. He does deals with some of the wealthiest families like the Hiltons, Rockefellers, Vanderbilts, Greg Norman and many others.

This guy has connections that most people only dream about. And he gets in on the same deals these guys are doing. Lucky for us, he opens them up for his inner circle of investors, and he opens them up for Barefoot Retirement clients. I only wish I would have found this guy 19 years ago. It would have saved me a ton of heartache and red ink.

It Gets Even Better: 1 + 1 = 3

So, as if this connection wasn't good enough, as fate would have it, I happened to run into an old friend of mine at a conference I was speaking at in Dallas. Do you know that feeling you get when you meet and talk with someone, and you just *KNOW* it's right? You get that feeling like it was meant to be. Well, that was exactly what it was like. This friend of mine was involved with what I believe to be the finest retirement vehicle ever created. No exaggeration, no hype. Truly, it's that good and I'll prove it to you! It was so good, in fact, the company that created it has patents pending on the program and has limited its use and availability only to exclusive providers.

Before I give you all the details of this amazing program, let me tell you just some of the benefits it offers. Trust me, you won't find a better program out there, anywhere!

(Note: Variations of this program have been around for over 150 years, but our patented version of this program is less than a year-old. It uses many of the core elements of the programs used in the past, but the patent-pending innovations it has makes it many, many times better than any other similar program out there.)

Remember Joe DiMaggio's famous quote, *"It ain't braggin' if ya can back it up?"* We can definitely back all of this up. It's the real thing.

You're going to discover that this is the best way to stockpile cash, and build true wealth, in a completely tax-free environment!

Take a Look At Some Facts About This Amazing Program.

» **Used by Presidents** - John F. Kennedy, Franklin D. Roosevelt, Presidents Taft, Cleveland, McKinley, and Harding all had these types of accounts. Even Joe Biden has an account like this.

» **Used by some of the Wealthiest Families in America** – Walt Disney, JC Penney, Rothschild family, Rockefeller family, Ray Kroc (McDonald's founder), Doris Christopher (Pampered Chef founder) are just some of the people who used this program to grow or save their fortunes.

» **Used by some of the Largest Banks in the World** – Citibank has 4.5 billion in these types of accounts, JP Morgan Chase has 9.8 billion, Wells Fargo has over 19.4 billion invested in these accounts. There are over 4,000 banks that have over 140 billion invested in these types of accounts.

» **Used by some of the Largest Companies in the World** – Wal-Mart, GE, Comcast, Johnson & Johnson, Harley-Davidson, Disney, Verizon, Gannett and almost 700 other Fortune 1,000 companies all have these types of accounts.

We know we're among good company, but it gets even better.

The Barefoot Retirement Plan has all of these benefits as well.

» **Tax-Free** – This program provides 100% TAX-FREE income. You are protected from *ALL* future tax increases.

» **No Limits to Annual Contribution Amounts** -- This is huge! (Subject to qualifications.)

» **No Distribution Penalties** – You can take any amount of your money out, anytime you want it, at any age, for any reason, all 100% penalty free.

» **No Investment Restrictions Or Prohibited Transactions** – You can invest in ANYTHING you wish.

» **Never Decreases in Value Due to Market Downturn** – You participate in upside growth and totally eliminate downside risk! (You will sleep better.)

» **No Mandatory Minimum Required Distributions** – Don't want to be forced to start taking your money out at age 70 ½? No problem. Take out what you want, when you want. You have complete control.

» **Creditor Proof** – If you're ever sued or face bankruptcy, your funds may be protected, safe and sound. Creditors don't even have the right to ask about this in most states.

» **Completely PRIVATE**- There is zero Government or IRS reporting required at all. None!

» **Potential For Lifetime, Tax-Free Income** – When structured and funded properly, this program can pay you for life, tax-free. We can show you how.

» **Leverage or Double Dipping** – *This is the best part of the program.* You have the option to earn a zero to 17% return each year, (depending on market index performance), and while still earning that return, you can choose to take those same funds and invest them in other areas, giving you the potential to earn a DOUBLE return on the exact same money! More on this in a moment.

» **Backed and Protected by the Government** – Even though this is the single best way to legally avoid paying taxes, this program is protected by its own section in the tax code. Government officials, politicians, bureaucrats and even Presidents have used this method to protect their own money from taxes.

WOW! Why Haven't I Heard Of This Before?

This sounds almost too good to be true. Why haven't I heard of this before? Well, don't feel bad. Only about one person in several thousand has even heard of this concept before. The

Government actually places tight restrictions on the advertising of these accounts, even though they're 100% legal.

Plus, only a very, very few, specialty trained advisors are participating in our patented program and very few of them have the specialized knowledge and contacts to set up it properly and maximize its potential earning power.

In a moment, I'm going to tell you how we're able to maximize the returns on this amazing patented retirement program and then have the option to reinvest those same funds into some of the amazing programs that my friend mentioned above, offers his insiders, and more. And…I'll even tell you about another program with a 12% annual return that is backed by rock-solid collateral.

The Biggest Secret in the Financial Industry

As you discover more about this amazing strategy, you'll find it's probably the best-kept secret in the entire financial industry. What we discovered was shocking. This strategy is like having your own Capital Warehouse or bank. And as you will soon see, **it's one of the SAFEST places on earth to keep your retirement funds.** That's why so many of the world's financial elite and even the bankers are putting so much of their money in these programs today.

> "This program has become a tax shelter for the rich… it gives the affluent tax advantages far beyond those available to middle-income people through a 401(k) or IRA."
> ~The Wall Street Journal

Yes, it's true that some people are putting millions of dollars a year into these programs. Lucky for us, the same opportunity is available for just about any investor. In fact, if funds are tight, you can start with as little as $300 a month. This program allows you to invest like the wealthy invest, even if you're not wealthy… yet! It doesn't matter if you are rich, poor, young, old, married, single, healthy, unhealthy — just about anyone in American can choose to take advantage of this amazing opportunity.

The Secret Savings Account of the Rich and Corporate America

Are you concerned about the banking sector? Concerned that the 2008 stock market and banking sector crash was just a prelude to much larger things to come? **You will soon discover that the retirement program I'm going to be showing you is one of the safest business and savings programs on earth.**

The Barefoot Retirement Plan Revealed

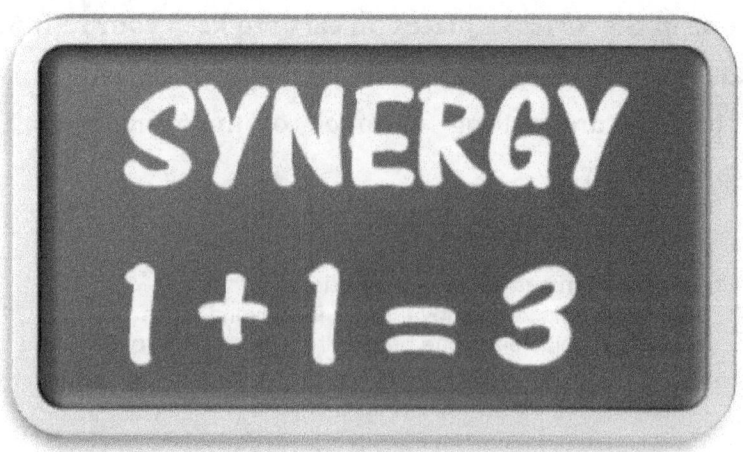

The Barefoot Retirement Plan is made up of 2 parts. You can choose to participate in part 1 or in part 2. Or, if you want to really maximize your retirement options, you can participate in BOTH parts. You will see how they work together in a moment. If you choose to participate in both parts, you'll be using the same investment principals that are usually reserved for the ultra-rich, but are now made available to average investors through this plan.

If you're an avid Shark Tank viewer like I am, I'm sure you've seen Kevin O'Leary or Mr. Wonderful. Here's one of his famous quotes, *"Here's how I think of my money: As soldiers. I send them out to war every day. I want them to take prisoners and come home, so there's more of them."*

If you choose to utilize both parts of this plan, you will have the opportunity to have your money work double-duty overtime for you. Your money has the ability to earn returns in two different places at one time. It's really brilliant.

Part 1 is Called the Guaranteed Index Account (GIA)

It's completely outside of the banking sector

Its history goes back to 1759

Options for guaranteed returns, solid track record of being the safest savings vehicle on earth

100% tax-free if set up and used correctly

Part 2 is Called the Outside Investment Accelerator or (The Power of Leverage)

Option to deploy the same funds into two different investments at the same time.

Otherwise known at double-dipping or arbitrage.

Option for high-yielding hard assets

Option to own the most-used commodity on earth

Reliable returns

First, we will explain part 1, then part 2. Next we'll show you how to combine both of them for maximum leverage and benefits.

CHAPTER 11

Part 1:
The Guaranteed Index Account

Here's the key to The Barefoot Retirement Plan. It's based off of a little known unique variation of an asset that has been in existence for over 150 years called dividend-paying life insurance.

It's all made possible by a congressionally approved IRS Tax Code # 7702 that allows us to have all the amazing benefits of the Guaranteed Index Account mentioned above through the use of Indexed Universal Life. Otherwise known as an IUL. Who would have thought that the Government allows all of these benefits through the use of Index Universal Life? However, keep in mind, **this is NOT like *anything* else you've ever seen.**

So yes, we are talking about a form of life insurance. But it's a highly specialized form of insurance. What we're doing is using a form of permanent life insurance as a savings vehicle the same ways the largest banks in the world are using it.

Don't be surprised if you've never heard of it. As a general rule, most insurance agents, financial planners, financial media *"experts"* and stock brokers don't have a clue about this nor do they even come close to understanding it. The masses know nothing about this. You know what they say, *"If you follow the masses, you'll end up in the same place as the masses."* Believe me, retirement wise… you don't want to end up where the masses are.

The first thing that pops into a lot of people's heads is something like this, *"Hey, my brother-in-law sells insurance, so I'll talk with him about this and see what he thinks."* That's fine, but keep this in mind.

Probably less than 1 in a thousand insurance agents has even heard of this concept and far, far fewer of them have any specialized knowledge about this at all. Plus, this specific product is 100% EXCLUSIVE to our private distribution channel. Anyone outside of our distribution channel CANNOT offer this program and does not have access to it.

Out of approximately 1,000 major life insurance companies, only a small handful of them offer policies that have features similar to the ones we offer. When you couple this with the fact that there are advertising limitations on these types of policies and with the fact that agents typically make 50% to 70% less commission when selling these policies, it's easy to understand why most people have never heard of this.

The Single Most Powerful Tax-Strategy Legally Allowed in America.

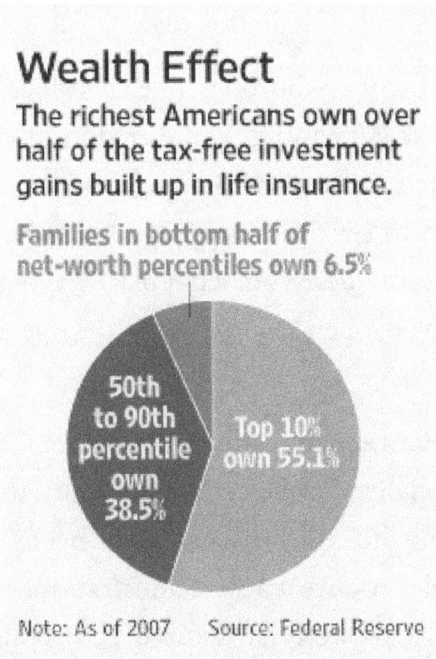

As you can see in this pie chart created by the Federal Reserve, the top 10% of the wealthiest Americans own over 55% of some form of this type of insurance. Furthermore, not shown on the chart but reported in the Federal Reserve findings was the fact that the wealthiest 1% own 22% of this type of insurance. That tells you a lot right there. The average person is never going to hear about the strategies the rich use to grow their wealth.

> The Barefoot Retirement Plan is all about taking the most effective wealth strategies that have primarily been used by the rich, and making them available to everyone.

Setting up one of these policies is a lot like going to a medical specialist. If you have a problem with your heart, you're not going to go to a general practitioner, right? You're going to go to a heart specialist. You wouldn't go ask your brother-in-law about your heart, unless of course, he/she happened to be a heart specialist. The same is true in this case.

If you go to someone who does not specialize in this form of IULs, you can risk everything. There are lots of variables, options and sophisticated strategies that need to be considered and specifically used to set these up properly. If they are not set up correctly, you can open yourself up to having the policy fail altogether or even open yourself up to large unnecessary tax liabilities.

Our Barefoot Retirement team specializes in setting up these unique and specialized policies. We're happy to schedule a free strategy session with you, discuss your needs and options in great detail and produce various illustrations that will clearly show you how a properly structured IUL policy can have an amazingly positive impact on your retirement. It can even allow you to have a barefoot lifestyle retirement, living life on your own terms.

To Schedule a Free, Private Consultation, Get Your Questions Answered And Have Custom Illustrations Run For You:
Call Us : (866) 480-7784
Email Us: info@BarefootRetirement.com
Complete A Request Form At: www.BarefootRetirement.com/schedule

What Do Other Financial Experts Think of This Type of Program?

Fox Business published an article by Scott Mann titled **"(Legally) Cutting Out the Tax Man in Retirement.** The article states, *"The life insurance industry has the best IRS-approved retirement savings plan today—, and most investors know nothing about it." "Despite sales of well over $1 Billion in 2011 for the top 39 carriers surveyed,* **it is the financial industry's No. 1 secret—Indexed Universal Life (IUL)."**

The article went on to say, *"To explain why IUL is a powerful supplemental savings vehicle to an employer's 401(k) plan, and a replacement for those whose employers don't offer one or for some people who don't trust the market, we need to start with the fact that after a generation of use, qualified plans - comprised of equity-based investments - are generally acknowledged as failures."*

Fox Business published an article by Tim Fussell titled, **"Is There Really A Perfect Life Insurance Contract?"** The article concluded that there was no one perfect policy that can solve everyone's needs and there are trade offs with each one. However, it went on to say, *"But an emerging and fast-growing contract design - the indexed universal life (IUL) policy - may come very close to being the ideal contract for most consumers in today's interest and overall market environment."*

Timothy R. Fussell also published another excellent article on Fox Business titled, **"Indexed Universal Life Insurance Policies: The Perfect Option for Professionals and Business Owners."**

In this article, he states, *"For a professional such as a doctor, attorney or CPA, the Indexed Universal Life policy is perfect for your retirement needs. Often as a professional, you operate as a P.A. being taxed as a sole proprietor, an S Corporation or a C Corporation, and under the tax codes you are limited to retirement account choices. The SEP IRA, Solo-401k or the UNI-401k, all allow you to save on a tax-deferred basis; but the maximum contribution limit is still the same, $49,000."*

"Now let's explore the IUL (indexed universal life) and why it is a better choice. As a professional of these types, your income level is much higher than average, so you max out your contribution very early in the year. With the IUL, there is no limit on how much money you can contribute…"

So How and Why Is Our Plan So Different?

You may have heard of a variation of this concept before. It's sometimes called things like; Bank On Yourself, Becoming Your Own Banker, a 770 Account, Tax-Free Retirement, etc. The HUGE majority of plans like this rely on a form of Whole Life Insurance. **The *"special"* version of Indexed Universal Life (IUL) that we use for our program is vastly different and easily outperforms these other plans by a mile.** I mean it's not even close, and we'll prove it to you in black and white.

Most of these other insurance policies focus on the Death Benefit. While that's important, and it's definitely part of our program, it makes the insurance part of the policy *VERY EXPENSIVE.*

When an insured person dies, all the other life insurance policies are structured to offer beneficiaries a choice of a **Lump Sum Payout <u>OR</u> Payments Over Time.** It's just been that way for well over a hundred years, and it has always worked well. So if someone died with a million-dollar life insurance policy, the beneficiary could choose to either take the million dollars in a lump sum, all at one time, OR they could choose to receive payments over time, per a schedule they choose for payments.

If you were the insurance company, you would need to accrue to have the million dollars available to give the beneficiary if they choose the lump sum option, and it's very expensive to do that. However, if the insurance company did not have to make that lump sum of money available, they could keep that million dollars invested in other, longer term, productive assets and growing much faster.

A very wise man who is part of our association came up with a brilliantly simple idea that changed everything. He developed this concept; IF you did not give the beneficiary an option to choose a lump-sum payment, and only gave them the option to receive payments over time, this one little change would greatly reduce the cost of insurance and thus allow clients to put a much greater amount of capital to work for them, growing their retirement assets even more.

This may seem like a small thing, but the results it yields are huge! You'll see just how huge it can be shortly, when we show you some scenarios.

This little change can reduce the cost of the insurance by up to 70%! That makes this type of IUL MUCH Less Expensive.

(Note: If the policy holder wishes, we can still structure an IUL policy that does offer a lump sum payout if they choose it, but it does make the cost of insurance greater. We have the flexibility to structure any type of insurance program that best suits our client's individual needs.)

Trust me when I tell you how much less expensive our choice is. Many of the people out there who sell Whole Life Insurance are quick to tell you theirs is similar in price. It's not. Not by a long shot. If you are considering a Whole Life product or ANY other type of insurance product, I challenge you to carefully compare prices. You will be shocked at the difference! Ours offers much more value and benefits, for much less cost! **Our version of IUL is like buying a Lamborghini at bargain basement costs.**

This concept was so revolutionary, they patented it.

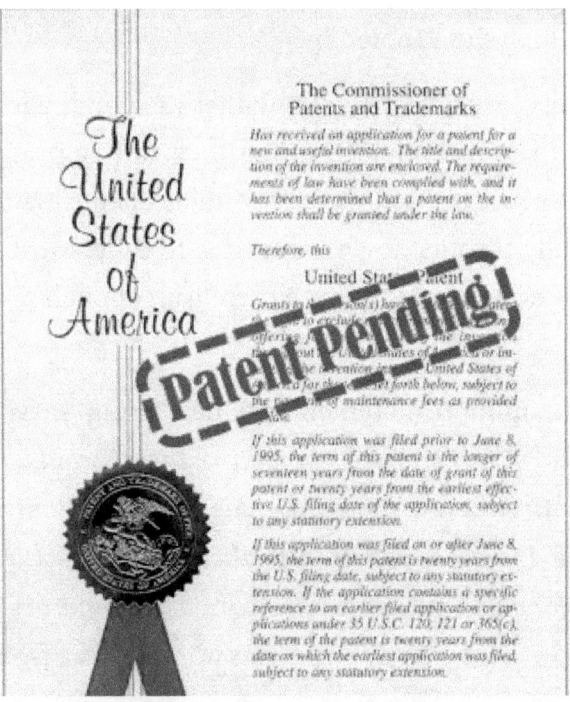

> That's another reason why the odds of you having heard about this special type of IUL policy are so slim. This specialized program has only been available for less than a year, and while it's still under patent, only a very small, select group of specialized agents have the ability to offer it.
>
> There are thousands of other agents, chomping at the bit to be able to have the ability to offer this product. It's that good!
>
> The unique thing about this specialized type of IUL policy is that it offers the VERY BEST VALUE for the **CLIENT**, and not the agent.

You may have heard one of the complaints about the *"regular"* type of Whole Life Policies is that the agents make a TON of money on them. It's true. Agents make a lot of commissions on them, and I'm sure you know; those commissions come from somewhere, right?

When agents sell the specialized type of policy that we are talking about here, they usually make **50% to 75% LESS,** than the guys selling the Whole Life.

Almost every week we meet with other insurance agents who are interested in joining our team, so they can gain access to this specialized program and offer it to their clients. Sadly, a few of them actually turn us down from time to time. Most of the ones who turn it down do so because there isn't enough profit in it for them.

The most common statement we hear from these people is, *"Why would I want to sell something that I would make up to 75% less on? Are you nuts? My clients will buy anything I sell them, and I would rather sell them a product that's more profitable for me. I've got to take care of me and my family, not theirs."* Wow! Not exactly what you want to hear from an agent, right?

By the way, if you're an insurance agent reading this book, and you don't mind putting your clients' needs first and earning a lower commission to be able to offer them the finest product they will ever see, give us a call. We license other agents and agencies all the time.

Our philosophy is and always has been 100% customer focused. We always put our customer's needs FIRST, and then everything else works out. Just like my old friend Zig Ziglar used to say, **"You can get everything in life you want, if you will just help enough other people get what they want."**

Besides, if we can give our clients a superior product, that's a far better value than anyone else can offer, they'll tell their friends and bring us referral customers, and that's the way we want it.

IRR (Internal Rate of Return)

Policies like IULs and Whole Life policies have a rating system called an IRR or Internal Rate of Return. When you look at the IRR, it's like looking underneath the hood of that car you are considering purchasing. It shows you how the policy will perform, based on the assumptions you've made and the other variables such as age, amount invested, and years until withdrawal, estimated market returns, etc.

If you are considering purchasing a Whole Life policy, ask the agent to give you the IRR of the policy you're considering. Sometimes it may be difficult to get them to show this to you. Do you know why? It's because their IRR compared to their illustrated rate of return isn't so hot. We will gladly give you this information because we know ours is superior and can't be beat! We're proud to show this and give it to you.

Our cost of insurance is the lowest you will find for programs like this. There are even ways we can structure your policy where your cost of insurance can completely stop. When that happens, one of your largest internal costs is removed, and your IRR goes through the roof. That's why our program can't be beat.

It's Like Having a Life Insurance Plan and a Savings Plan, Rolled Into One Plan

This program truly gives you the best of both worlds. You get very affordable permanent life insurance to take care of your family, and you also get tax-free income for retirement. This plan offers you the best combination of safety, flexibility, guarantees, control, liquidity, and tax advantages that's ever been created. *It helps you Protect, Grow and Leverage your retirement savings.*

The specialized IUL product we offer outperforms the competition by drastically increasing the internal efficiency of the policy. By increasing the efficiency, it means you have a lower expense ratio, a higher account value, and significantly higher amounts you can take as income distributions.

How Safe and Secure Are the Life Insurance Companies That Issue This Type of IUL?

That's a very important question. Let's break it down and look at it. There are basically two different types of insurance companies. Stock companies and Mutual companies.

Stock Companies: Stock companies are publicly traded. They must always have their *"shareholders"* best interest in mind more-so than their policy holders. They must focus on the short-terms demands of Wall Street, and their values are subject to the ups and downs of the stock market.

Mutual Companies: Mutual insurance companies are not publicly traded and do not have stocks or shareholders. They pay out their profits in the form of dividends to their policy holders. They always have their <u>policy holder's</u> long-term best interest in mind. The payout of dividends is not guaranteed, however, of all the mutual insurance companies that we work with, not one of them has missed a single payment, EVER.

Most of these companies are over a hundred years old, and they are among the financially strongest companies in the world. Warren Buffet is even on record for saying that this business model of mutual insurance companies is one of the safest businesses in the world. In 2008 during the banking crisis studies indicate that 12% of banks failed and only .08% of life insurance companies failed.

The primary company we work with for our flagship IUL product is a mutual insurance company and has been in business since the 1880s (over 130 years). They have over a trillion dollars in force that protects 13 million customers nationwide. Their stellar record of financial strength and claims-paying ability positions them as **one of the most highly rated companies in America.** So the issuing company is as solid of a company that you would ever hope to work with.

In the book **Money, Bank Credit and Economic Cycles**, the author Jesus Huerta de Soto reported that, *"In the last two hundred years, a negligible number of life insurance companies have disappeared due to financial difficulties."* In his book, he contrasts this to the high *'financial death rate'* of banks, which can systematically suspend their payments and can fail without the support of the central banks.

We simply don't think you can find a safer place on Planet Earth for your retirement funds!

CHAPTER 12

How It Works

So Let's Walk Through the Steps of Exactly How It Works

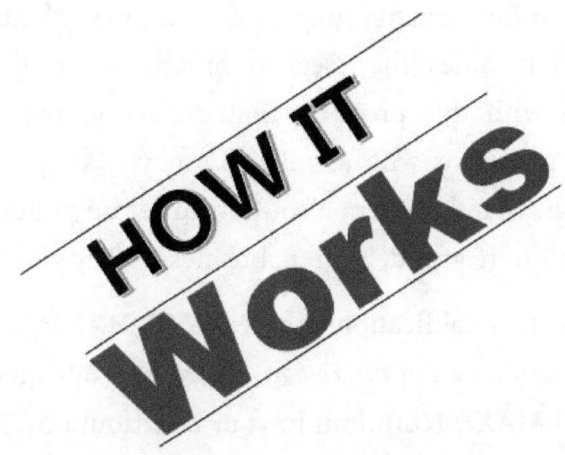

Getting Started

Getting started is actually very easy. You consult with one of our highly specialized Barefoot Retirement agents. We look at your specific situation, your goals, desires, needs, wants, resources, etc. and give you advice on creating a custom-tailored plan that best suits your individual needs. This is NOT a *"cookie cutter"* program. There are lots of variables and options available, and our highly trained specialist will work with you to structure a plan that perfectly meets your needs and helps you achieve your goals.

Some of our plans are structured for contributions to be made each year, for 5 to 7 years. (We can structure programs with much longer contribution time periods if that best suits your needs). You would also determine the amount of contributions that you wish to make on a monthly, quarterly or annual basis. Typically, the minimum contribution amount is about $300/month or $3,600 per year.

Our Barefoot Retirement group works with many high net worth clients. Often times they see so much power, benefits and advantages with this program that do everything possible to fund their programs with as much money as they can possibly put together. Many of them also want to set up policies for their spouses, children, grandchildren, businesses, key employees, etc.

Based on your qualifications, there is **NO MAXIMUM** limit to your contributions. *Let me repeat.* Based on your qualifications, there is **NO MAXIMUM** limit to your contributions. *Really! Our clients love this!*

In most other cases, when you're buying insurance primarily for the death benefit, you look for ways to put as *little* into a policy as you can. This is the opposite. Once you understand the massive power of what we are talking about here, you'll be looking hard to see just how much you can put into this program to max it out. It really is that good!

There are many great people who love this program, but have limited financial assets. As part of our mission, we're determined to help as many Americans as we possibly can, to obtain and achieve the Barefoot Retirement they want and deserve. Many people see this program as the answer to their prayers, but they just don't have much unallocated funds sitting around to start their IUL with. So, if you're struggling to find ways to come up with the money to fund your IUL, we have some ideas for you.

10 Ideas for Finding the Money for Your IUL

Note: Before you make any financial moves, it's always recommended that you seek professional guidance from specialists who are knowledgeable in these specific areas. We do not give financial advice. These are simply ideas that you may want to consider and do more research on.

1. **Re-allocate under-performing assets**
   Many times people have under-performing assets in their portfolio that could be better utilized. Why? Because it's nearly impossible to keep your portfolio 100% efficient. If you have some *"dead"* assets that have not been performing up to par, and are not helping you to reach your financial goals, you may consider using those funds. It's kind of like the old saying, *"What have you done for me lately?"*

2. **Reduce your funding of your IRA, or 401(k)**
   After seeing all the advantages this program offers, many people can't wait to reduce or stop their funding of their qualified plans. However, if your employer offers a

matching amount, you could consider paying only the amount up to the employer matching level.

3. **Use some of the funds in your IRA, or 401(k)**
   There is a Federal rule that's called the 72(t). This section in the tax code allows you to pull money out of your traditional qualified retirement plan. By using the 72(t) option, you avoid the 10% penalty that's usually assessed when you move funds out of qualified plans. This only applies to people younger than 59 ½. Before making a move like this, be sure to talk with a knowledgeable tax and financial professional.

4. **Better management of your home equity**
   Some people make extra payments to their home mortgage every month. It's easy to re-allocate those funds to an IUL. Depending on your mortgage, you may consider refinancing your loan to free up some extra funds. For many, this is their largest expense so it's a good place to look for savings.

5. **Convert your current life insurance policy**
   Some people have been *"sold"* really bad and underperforming life insurance policies over the years. In fact, I bet if you were to check the IRR (Internal Rate of Return) on your policy, you may be in for a shock. This is not always a good idea to do, and you should always seek professional advice before making a move like this.

   If this seems like your best option, you can take advantage of a 1035 Exchange to transfer the cash value of your current policy to your new policy. Our Barefoot Retirement advisors are happy to look at your old policy and run some illustrations that will show the pros and cons of making a move. They will then discuss the advantages and disadvantages with you so you will have all the facts to make an informed decision.

6. **Restructuring debt**

    If you have some personal or business debt that requires a good portion of your monthly cash flow, you could look into possibly restructuring some of the debt to free up some additional funds.

7. **Savings accounts**

    If you have some portion of your savings accounts sitting around in bank savings accounts earning 0.12% or in CDs earning not much more than a percent or two, you may consider moving some of your savings into an IUL account. If the market continues to perform as it has over the past few decades, you're likely to earn much more on those funds. Plus, you can purchase a rider on your policy that will give you almost immediate access to borrow the majority of those funds, should you need them.

8. **Reducing your current monthly expenses**

    This is an area that in the past, many people didn't want to talk about. However, with the seriousness of having a properly funded retirement, many people become remarkable creative in finding ways to cut back and reduce unnecessary monthly expenses. For some, it's as simple as keeping your car a few years longer after it's paid off. Others are reducing their vacation costs, eating out less, going to the movies less, and just buying fewer new & shiny objects that simply aren't really necessary.

9. **Part-time job**

    We know this doesn't work for everyone, but for some, it can be a perfect solution. Depending on your financial situation, this could be the smartest thing you could do. For most, it will be easier to pick up a part-time job now, while you're younger and healthier, than it would be when you are much older, and you just don't have the stamina to go back to work. For some, it's short-term pain now, to ensure a long-term gain later.

One of our clients is a pharmacist. He absolutely loved this program and could easily afford to contribute a significant amount on funds to it on an annual basis. We ran various illustrations for him, showing him lots of retirement options. After seeing just how amazing his retirement ***could be*** with this program, if he really contributed to this program in a big way, he decided to pick up a part-time pharmacy job for the next 5 years.

His view of how his retirement would be before he saw this program, was just *"okay."* After he realized just how powerful, the Barefoot Retirement program really is, he decided to make a short-term sacrifice, in return for having a vastly different retirement. With his new retirement plan, he should now be able to retire at 60 (or sooner) instead of 65, and have a *significantly larger* annual lifetime retirement income than he ever imagined.

10. **Make changes to your annual tax refund**

    If you are one of those people who typically gets a large tax refund, you may want to consider using that to fund your IUL. When the IRS gives you that large tax refund each year, they are really just giving you back the money on an interest-free loan that you've given them all year long. They are just giving you your own money back that THEY have had the benefit of using. If this sounds like you, you can first check with your tax advisor and then make some simple withholding adjustments to your W-4 at work. Don't worry, you can make changes to your W-4 as often as you wish. By making this change you can often immediately free up some extra monthly cash flow that you can use for your IUL.

Missing Contributions

Many of the standard Whole Life policies out there are highly structured, and if you miss a payment contribution, or some payments, in some cases it can even destroy the integrity and value of your entire policy. **This is a really, really big deal!**

Our IUL program is DIFFERENT. If you miss a contribution here or there, no problem. You can simply make it up later. ***These plans are extremely flexible.*** There are three contribution amounts you can choose from. You can mix and match these from year to year, even month to month! There is a minimum, a maximum, and a Target.

The Target is what insurance companies tell you that you need to keep the death benefit in force through your lifetime. This isn't the number we want to use for maximum efficiency. The minimum is the bare minimum you can contribute over a given time period (monthly or yearly). The maximum, in how we structure these plans, is the maximum amount the IRS will allow you to put into the policy based on the amount of death benefit you select.

Don't worry if you find this confusing. We walk you step-by-step through every aspect to help you stay on course and maximize your policy. It's really very simple once you understand it.

Using After Taxed Dollars

You fund your IUL with after taxed dollars. These are funds that you've already paid taxes on. As you know, with a *"qualified"* retirement program like an IRA or a 401(k), you fund those programs with before taxed dollars.

That's the big *"claim to fame"* of qualified programs and what they brag so much about. They tell you how great it is that you make your contributions with pre-taxed money, so you can pay less in taxes *now* and invest more funds *now*.

What they don't focus on is the little fact that you WILL have to pay taxes on *ALL* the funds when you start withdrawing them during your retirement. *That's right.* With qualified plans like IRAs & 401(k) s, when you start drawing your money out, you will have to pay taxes on the initial amount you invested *AND* on **ALL OF YOUR GAINS**.

Fact: You Don't Own All of Your 401(k)

Your Current Tax Rate
33%

If Taxes Go Up … You'll Own Even LESS

Your Future Tax Rate
39% ???

So let's think about this for a moment and see which way seems smarter. Let's use a simple general example to help understand the difference. Say you wanted to put $100,000 in your retirement account, and you were at the 28% tax bracket. If you are putting it into an IRA or 401(k), you pay no up-front tax on that 100k. It all goes into your retirement account. However, if you contribute to an IUL account, you would need to have close to $140,000 and pay the tax on that amount upfront, to be able to net the $100,000 to put into your IUL.

Now let's just say that you invested well and that when you reach retirement age, your account has grown to be worth 1 million dollars. If you had put it into an IRA or 401(k), you would have to pay taxes on **ALL** the money you take out, every single penny of it.

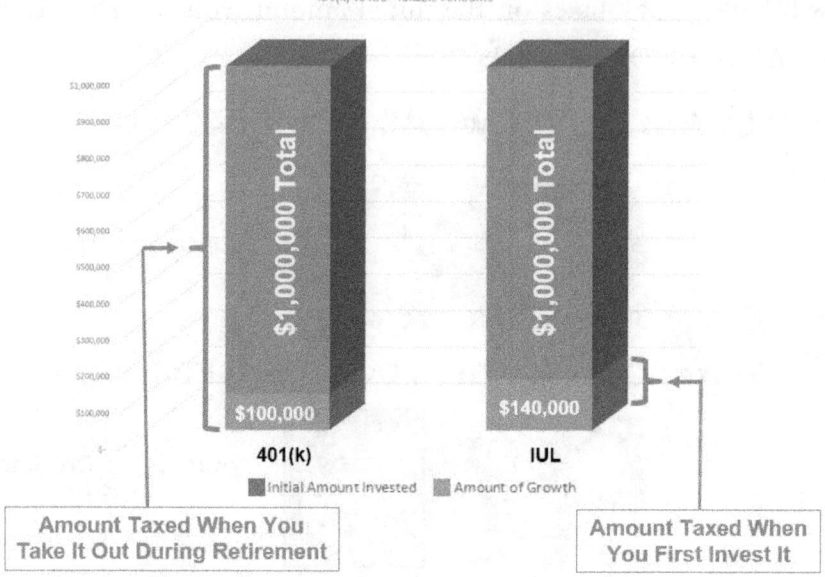

And, who knows what the tax rates will be when you get ready to retire. Not a single knowledgeable person I talk with about this believes taxes will be lower in the future. They all believe taxes will be higher. Much higher, not lower.

However, for this example, let's just say tax rates stay the same, and you're at the 28% tax bracket throughout the entire time period you withdraw your retirement funds to live on.

28% of 1 million dollars is $280,000. So that's a bit more than the additional $40k we had to pay in taxes initially to fund our IUL.

Would you rather pay Uncle Sam $40,000 today, or $280,000 when you retire?

Another way to look at this is as if you were a farmer. If you had the choice to pay taxes on your planting seeds or on your entire harvest, wouldn't you rather pay taxes on your small bags of planting seeds instead of paying taxes on your entire harvest?

You Get To Keep It ALL. It's 100% Tax-Free!

This Is How Much Of Your Retirement Funds You Will Get To KEEP If You Choose This Program.

The Future Tax Rate Does Not Matter

Plus, most people are going to need all the funds they can get during retirement. Who knows what kinds of unforeseen medical expenses, etc. will arise? It seems cruel to me that the Government steps in at a time when most people can least afford to part with their money, and collects *their* share of people's retirement funds.

Now That Our IUL Account Is Funded, What Happens Next?

Death Benefit – The Life Insurance Portion

First off, you can have the additional peace of mind knowing that in addition to having put investment funds into the finest retirement programs in the world, you also have a fantastic life insurance policy, with a great death benefit for your family should something happen to you. Some of our clients look at this as an added perk and others look at it as a critical aspect of this program.

When you compare putting your funds into a qualified plan like an IRA or a 401(k), versus putting them into our unique version of an IUL, having the death benefit in place is a great extra benefit that you just don't get with the other qualified programs. The IUL is like having life insurance and an iron-clad savings account, all rolled into one.

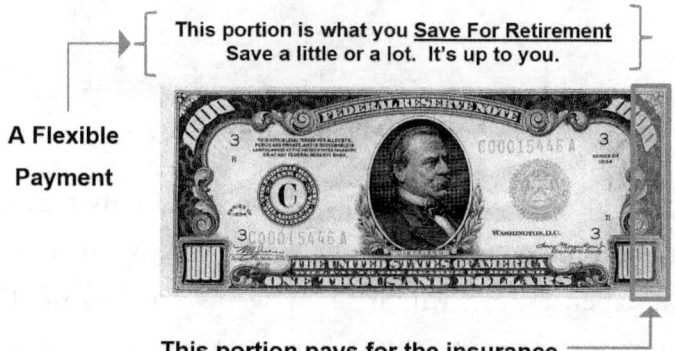

Death Benefit

Let's say you put the $100,000 into a typical IRA or 401(k) account, and let your broker or advisor (or even yourself) invest it. What do you think they would say if you called them up the next day and said something like, *"Hey Bill, I was just wondering, you know the $100,000 you're managing for me in my IRA or 401(k)? I was just wondering, if I were to die prematurely, how much of a death benefit would my family receive from my investment?"*

I think you know what the answer would be, right? Your IRA or 401(k) would simply become part of your estate, and your heirs would only receive the actual value of the account, and not a penny more. Plus they would most likely have to pay taxes on those funds.

The IUL option offers a significant death benefit that's usually much, much larger than the amount you invest. So it's kind of like getting the death benefit as a bonus, for the exact same amount of funds invested.

While the death benefit proceeds are not estate-tax free (unless special types of trusts are set up in advance), they are **income tax-free**. If a policy holder has any loans out against his policy, (more on this shortly), his tax-free and interest-free loans received are paid off and then all remaining proceeds are paid to his beneficiary(s) income-tax free as the death benefit.

While most of our focus in this book is on the retirement aspect of this plan, let's not forget how significant the death benefit can be with an IUL. If you would like to have the numbers run for you so you can see exactly how much of a death benefit you could have with a properly structured IUL contact us, and we'll be happy to run various illustrations for you.

Now, let's do a quick comparison of this program to a typical IRA or 401(k).

Risks: If you put the $100,000 into a typical IRA or 401(k) account, you're still subject to all the ups and downs of the market, and you have full risk. You may be saying to yourself, but my broker or advisor is really watching it carefully. Haaa. Do you remember just how many of the guru super smart brokers and advisors totally got the market wrong in 2008? These were trained and experienced professionals who have access to the best data in the world, and most of them missed it by a mile and got creamed.

Do you really think they've learned from history and will avoid it next time? Do you think history repeats itself? If you are either running out of time or simply sick-and-tired of taking these gigantic hits to your retirement account, then this solution offers a much better alternative.

How Your Funds Increase In Value

As we have mentioned above, each IUL account is set up specifically for each individual's needs. For many accounts, we recommend that they choose a blended indexed account strategy. (We review all the options with you, and you choose the ones that are best suited for you). Plus, you can easily change your selections from time to time.

Our blended index is made up of the S&P 500 (35%), Russell 2000 (10%), Barclays Capital U.S. Aggregate Bond Index (35%), and EUROSTOXX50 (20%).

Each year, the cash value of your account gets credited with an amount of interest gain based on the performance of the blended index.

Just so we are clear here; your funds are not actually invested in the stock market nor in these indexes themselves. They are just credited with the performance gains of the index blend. Here's the REALLY GOOD PART....

You Can *NEVER* Lose Money Due to Market Downturns.

It's true. **When you use our flagship IUL product, you are 100% GUARANTEED to NEVER LOSE MONEY with your account due to market downturns.** To protect you, your money and your retirement, we have a guaranteed 0% base. We also have a 17% cap on returns. This is such an amazingly powerful part of the Barefoot Retirement Program. Let's look at an example to better understand this.

Let's say you have $100,000 in your IUL account, and you've chosen the blended index. Now, let's say the stock market and the S&P 500 index falls 38% like it did in 2008. No problem. You have a 0% guaranteed base so you can NEVER lose money. So at the end of that year, let's say the blended index was down 38%, your account would be credited 0%, or in other words, it would still be worth $100,000 (fewer internal expenses like cost of insurance in the early years). (However, you would NOT have sustained a 38% loss, and your account would not have gone down to $62,000.)

Now, let's say the next year, the market and the blended index value goes up 20%. At the end of the year, your account will be credited a 17% gain, or an additional $17,000 since we have a cap at 17%. So you may be thinking, yes… but I got jipped out of the additional 3%. *True, kind-of.* However, would you like to take a guess of how this works out over the long run? *Just wait until you see this next example.*

CHAPTER 13

S&P 500 vs IUL – Who Wins?

(Case study – You vs your cool brother-in-law Todd)

Don't skip this chapter – this is so powerful.

Let's take a look at an example of ACTUAL market performance over 15 years. *This is amazing!* The chart below compares the results of two different options. We use the actual S&P 500 historical returns from 1998, through 2012, to compare.

Let's say, for example, you are the green line on the chart and your cool brother-in-law Todd, is the red line. You both put in $100,000 in 1998. Todd chooses to put his funds into a 401(k), and invests it in the S&P 500 Index. Not a bad choice at all. You choose to put your funds into an IUL, and you select a blended index.

The market starts out moving upwards. Around year 2, Todd is doing great, and he's constantly bragging to you because his account is up to $151,409, and yours is only up to $136,890 due to the 17% cap on your account. So Todd thinks he's out smarted you again, and doesn't stop reminding you of it.

In the next few years, things start to change. The market has fallen, and at year 5, Todd's account has dropped to $90,664. *Yikes!* However, you aren't worried a bit, because your account is still at $136,890, due to the 0% cap you have. (You can't lose money due to market declines.)

When the market is in negative territory, you always preserve your gains. Unlike Todd, you never go below a 0% return due to market declines. You've noticed that Todd is pretty quiet these days. In fact, Todd looks a lot more stressed out these days. *And, you're sleeping much better than Todd is.*

Now let's go out 15 years. Todd's account has grown to a value of **$146,953.** You may be saying, *"That's not too bad."* After all, Todd's invested in the S&P 500, and the huge majority of mutual funds, and managed accounts produce lower returns than the S&P 500 typically does. So Todd was actually really smart for selecting the S&P 500. However, your little IUL account is up to **$316,499**. *Now who's looking like the really smart guy these days?*

> Your account is up **$169,546 MORE** than smarty pants Todd's account, and it's up about **115% MORE** than good ole Todd. Now, Todd rarely talks to you these days.

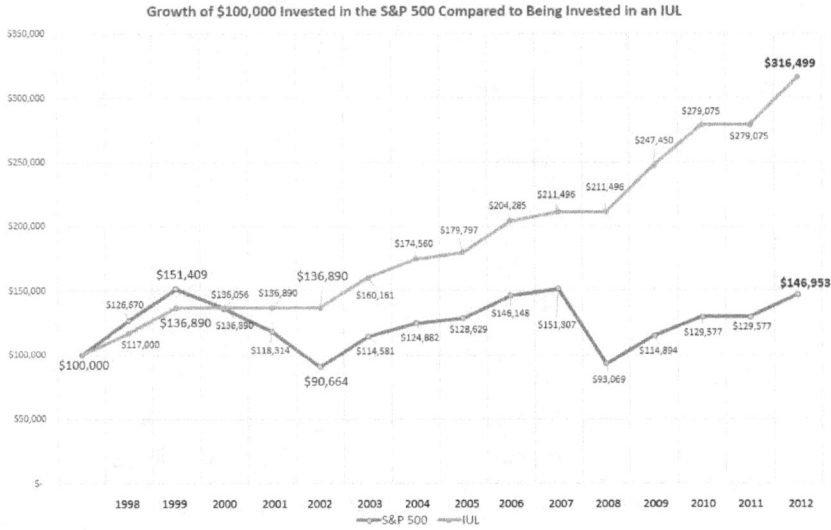

Key Points:

Notice the green line on the chart above. That's the one using the IUL. **The key point here to notice is that the green line *NEVER GOES DOWN*. Ever!** If the market goes UP, your gains go UP. If the market goes down, your line stays FLAT... but never goes down. Poor old Todd certainly can't say the same thing about his program.

Remember Warren Buffett's rules for investing? The rule is, if you want to be successful in the markets, *Never Lose Money*. The reason is, losing money kills your returns and takes a really long time to recover from losses. Just ask Todd. He'll tell you.

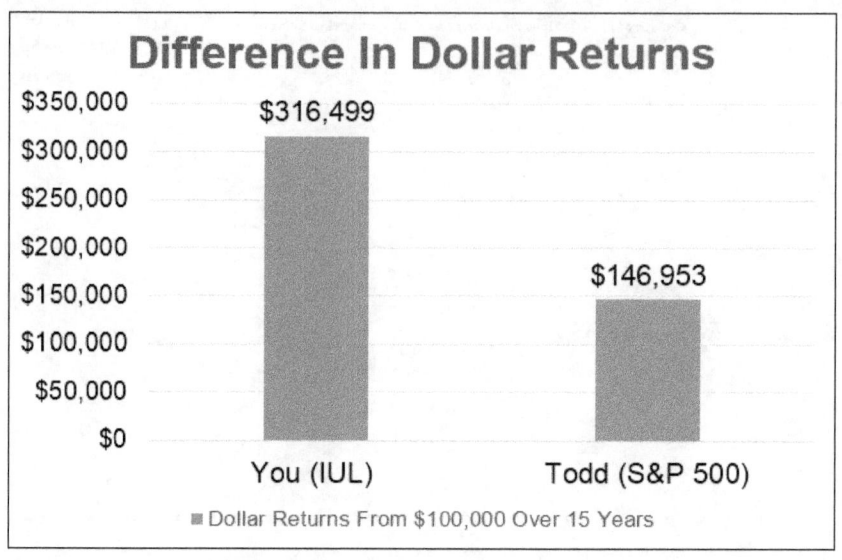

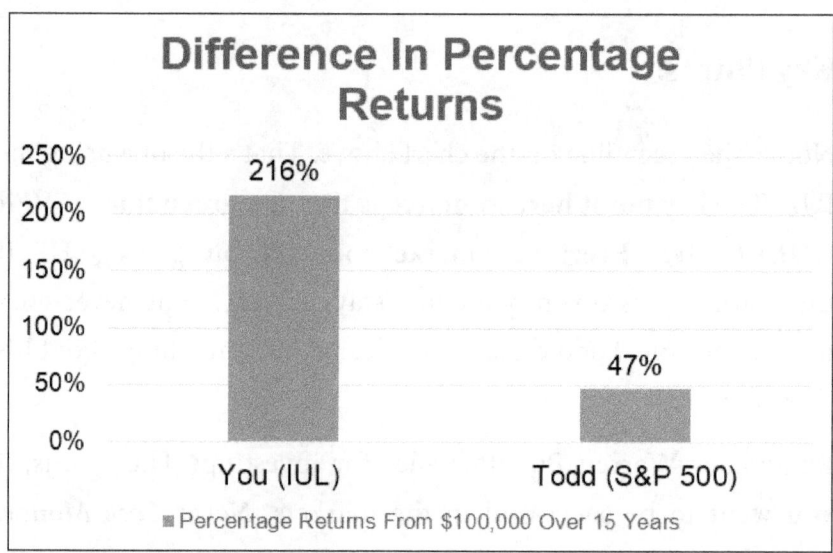

But wait, it gets better...

Genius Todd has to pay taxes on **ALL** the funds he takes out of his account. *All of them.*

You don't have to pay a single red cent in taxes on your funds. None. Zero. Zip. Nada.

So for simple math, if Todd had to pay 30% in taxes, he would only net out around $103,000. Wow!

When you compare the net spendable income (after taxes), between you and Todd, it's amazing. Todd has $103,000 to spend, and you have $316,499 to spend. So you have $213,499 MORE net funds to spend than Todd, because of a wise decision you made 15 years ago.

To be completely fair here, let's not forget this. Back 15 years ago, you <u>did</u> have to pay the taxes on the $100,000, before you put it into your IUL. Todd <u>did not</u> have to pay any taxes on the $100,000 he put into his 401(k), 15 years ago.

Now you're looking like a super genius. Your account net value is over 316k, and Todd's is only 103k. *(Now Todd doesn't even talk with you at Thanksgiving.)*

QUESTION: How much money did Todd invest 15 years ago?

Let's see; it seems like it was $100,000, right? So get this. Todd invested $100,000 15 years ago. He's sweated out all the white-knuckle ups and downs of the S&P 500 for 15 long years. He's watched the markets like a hawk, read every financial article and magazine he could get his hands on, and talked with his broker more often than he talks with his own brother.

However, after 15 long years, (after you take out the taxes), Todd ends up with the same stinking amount that he put in back when he started a decade and a half ago. (Does this sound familiar?)

And… that doesn't even account for **INFLATION** over all those years. If you go to usinflationcalculator.com and plug in 1998 to 2012, you'll see the inflation rate during that time was **40.9%**. Yikes! *Todd can't win for losing.*

Todd would have been better off putting his money in his mattress. *Amazing!*

And that's not all. Todd was at least smart enough to invest his money in the S&P 500. According to the Motley Fool, only 10 out of 10,000 actively managed mutual funds available, managed to beat the S&P 500 consistently, over the past 10 years. So you have to give Todd credit for making a much wiser investment decision than the big majority of investors. However, it's shocking to see how poorly he did.

Make no mistake about it. This is HUGE and can make all the difference in the world in you being able to enjoy the barefoot retirement of your dreams, or having to find a job to sustain yourself during retirement.

Plus, imagine how much better you'll sleep at night having the absolute 100% certainty that no matter what happens in the world, no matter what happens with the stock market; **your retirement account can NEVER lose money due to market downturns. Plus, you LOCK IN your gains, each year, so your**

account can NEVER be worth less than the previous year's value, due to market downturns. *This is a major benefit.*

CHAPTER 14

More Unbeatable Benefits

I'm sure you know the value of compounding. I love this quote:

"Compound interest is the eighth wonder of the world. He who understands it, earns it ... he who doesn't ... pays it." -- Albert Einstein

When you combine the power of compounding with Warren Buffet's #1 rule of never losing money, you get the perfect scenario with these types of accounts. They never lose money, and they compound year after year after year. Just take a look at these historical compound index account average returns. When you combine having zero risks and these kinds of returns, you get an unbeatable program.

Historical Compound Index Account Average Return

	From	To	Average Return with Growth Cap
10 Year	Dec 2004	Dec 2013	8.20%
15 Year	Dec 1999	Dec 2013	7.72%
20 Year	Dec 1994	Dec 2013	8.86%
24 Year	Dec 1990	Dec 2013	9.07%

This is a 9.07% average return over 24 years using this type of account with a 16% market index cap. (Note: They have recently raised the market index cap to 17%, and that change would bring the **24 year average return to 9.28 %**.) Obviously, no one knows what the future will bring nor what the market returns will be in the future. All we know for sure is this is what the returns have been in the past.

Fixed Return Option

If it would suit your individual needs better, you also have the option of selecting a FIXED rate of return each year.

At the time this is written, the current fixed return rate is approximately 3.5%. You can move in and out of the fixed rate account as often as you wish.

When selecting the index or blended index accounts, you can choose to move in and out of them once each year.

Ease of Operation

Setting up your IUL is pretty easy. You complete an application, work with a Barefoot Retirement advisor to design the plan that's right for you, have a medical screening, and fund your policy. That's pretty much all there is to it.

Once you get your account set up, it pretty much works on autopilot. There's really not much that you need to do, other than continue to fund your policy for the remaining years needed on your policy. You don't have to watch the stock market; you don't need to call your broker and worry about how all the crazy world events will impact your investments, and you don't have to make, buy and sell decisions.

You can just relax, spend time with your family, and go fishing, play golf, whatever you wish. You receive periodic account statements so you can monitor your account. Your agent is available to you at any time to answer any questions you have along the way.

Typically, we will schedule an annual phone consultation with you to discuss how your plan is progressing and see if any tweaks are needed, but there rarely are. Depending on market conditions, you may choose to switch from an indexed account to a fixed account, or vice versa. If you are taking loans from your account, we will review your account values and ratios to make sure you are making the right moves to keep your policy in good shape.

Is There Really No Maximum Or Cap On How Much I Can Put Into an IUL?

You do have to qualify for the policy. Both health wise (unless using the strategies mentioned above of insuring a spouse or a child) and from a financial standpoint. For example, if you make

50K a year, it's unlikely you will qualify for a 10 million-dollar policy.

However, if you are a qualified, high net worth individual, you may be surprised at just how much funds you will be able to sock-away into an IUL.

The unique aspect of this program is that once people fully understand the power and the benefits this program offers, they usually do everything they can to put every penny they can find into this program. Like we said before, *it's that good.*

Here's A Great Question For You:

If you could put your money into a program and:

- Have it grow from 0% to 17% per year
- Be 100% tax-free when you draw it out
- Be protected from litigation and bankruptcies
- Be completely and totally private and non-reportable
- Have the option to borrow against it anytime you wish
- Have the possibly earn a double return on the same funds

How much would you want to put into a program like this?

Allows You to Sleep Like a Baby

Can you just imagine how much better you will relax and sleep when you know 100% for sure that your retirement fund will NEVER lose money due to market declines? Ever!

These days all of us know in the back of our minds that we could wake up on any given day and find out a horrific terrorist event has taken place, or a massive war has broken out in the Middle East or Russia, or global oil supplies have been cut off, or our US Dollar has crashed or is no longer the World's Reserve Currency, or a million other scenarios that could take place on any given day.

(Most of us know that fears like this are more about WHEN they will happen than IF they will happen.)

You know if these types of events were to happen, they would most likely set off a global panic and send stock markets crashing. What if you were close to retirement, and most of your retirement funds that you are relying upon are in the markets? Can you afford to take that risk? Do you have the stomach for that risk? Do you have the endurance and/or time to try to fight your way back and recover from your losses after another Wall Street debacle?

Why subject yourself to the risk, uncertainty and the constant worry and fear if you don't have to? By simply making a decision to put some or all of your retirement funds in this IUL program, you can 100% insure your retirement fund from ever taking another loss again….PERIOD.

How many people have you seem who've had their lives ruined by the constant stress and worry about their money and retirement? Remember the pie chart earlier in the book that showed 61% of Americans feared running out of money during retirement more than they feared death? You now have a perfect solution for this. You can now totally and completely protect your retirement funds from ever taking a loss again, and you can greatly increase your quality of life and peace-of-mind at the same time.

Protection from Creditors, Lawsuits and Bankruptcies –

In many states, the cash value of your policy is totally and completely protected from all creditors. In some states, creditors don't even have the right to ask about these funds. Should you face a bankruptcy or lawsuit, you can relax and know that all the cash value funds in your policy are locked up, protected and safe and sound. This may not seem important to you at the moment, but if the unexpected were to arise, this benefit alone could make all the difference in the world in the quality of the retirement you will have.

This is especially meaningful for high-income earners in professions or businesses that are prone to lawsuits. Physicians, in particular, love this aspect of this plan. You can do everything right for your entire career, amass a huge retirement fund, and then have a malpractice suit that comes along and takes it all away.

When you couple the fact that you can put an unlimited amount of funds into this program AND keep them safe and protected from creditors, this benefit alone makes this program worth doing!

What If You Are Too Old Or In Poor Health?

This is a question we sometimes get. If a potential client is really getting up there in age, or sadly if they are in poor health and don't think they will be able to pass the medical exam that's given to all applicants to be sure they qualify for the life insurance policy, they are sometimes quick to want to give up and say, it's such a great program. Too bad I can't qualify.

We have lots of ideas and strategies that we use to help our clients. One option is to consider insuring a spouse or child who could qualify. You simply name yourself as the beneficiary of the policy, and you can get very similar benefits even though you're not the one actually insured.

Even if you're starting to get up there age-wise, don't worry. One of our partners coined this phrase:

> *"Our IUL makes a 60 year old look like a 50 year old!"*

If you're in doubt, the best thing to do is contact us and discuss your individual situation with one of our skilled advisors. They are trained to help you discover the best ways to help you maximize your retirement resources.

No Minimum Age or Income Requirement

Most qualified plans like IRAs, 401(k)s, ROTHs, SEP IRAs, etc. either require an amount of earned income or an age requirement before anyone can set up one of these programs. So if you are thinking about your young children, it's pretty hard for them to have an earned income when they are just little kids. This program is different! If you want to purchase an IUL for your children or grandchildren right after they are born, that's perfectly fine. No problem at all.

Image how much of a head start a child could get and how much further ahead they would be if an IUL was purchased for them when they were very young? You could give them a 20 year head start over other kids their age. Imagine having an extra 20 years for the funds to grow and compound and then be completely tax-free any time they choose to borrow them out.

No Mandatory Distribution

As you probably already know, the Government has strict rules that require you to start withdrawing your money out of qualified plans when you reach 70 ½. It does not make one bit of difference if you need the money at that time or not, the Government is going to force you to start pulling it out, or they are going to sock it to you with a 50% penalty. That's right. You either start withdrawing the required minimum distribution amount, or they are going to take 50% of that amount from you if you don't.

The reason the Government does this is because they want to get their hands on your money in the form of the taxes you will now have to start paying on the funds you draw out of your qualified plans. The Government figures they have waited long enough, and now it's time for them to start getting their money back from you. You either play by their rules, or they will start taking your money from you one way or another. Sounds pretty harsh doesn't it?

As you know by now, YOU are in complete control of your IUL. You can take your money out at ANY time you wish. You get to make up your own rules and don't have to be burdened by some arbitrary rules that bureaucrats came up with many decades ago that say when you need to start pulling your money out. They don't know your nor do they know or care about your individual needs. They just care about getting your money.

Why bother with all of that? The IUL gives you the freedom to live your life on your terms. If you need the money early on, no problem, just pull it out. If you choose to retire at 50 years old, no problem, you can start pulling it out then. If you don't need the money until you reach 100 years old, no problem. It's your money, your plan, your policy. You can do with it as you wish. That's the freedom that the Barefoot Retirement Plan gives you.

The IUL Does Not Create Taxation of Your Social Security Benefits

Many people are not aware of this, but a significant percentage of your Social Security benefits can be subject to income tax when you receive them. They compute the amount of income tax you owe based on WHERE your other retirement income comes from.

All of your money that comes from qualified plans like IRAs, 401(k)s, SEP IRAs, SIMPLE IRAs, etc., during your retirement WILL be included as additional income that can affect the amount of taxes you have to pay on your Social Security benefits. This can add up to a large amount of money.

The Government, however, does allow an exemption on this. The rules say, ALL income coming out of cash-value life insurance policies does NOT count as additional income that will affect the amount of taxes you will have to pay on your Social Security benefits. That's right. And it does not matter if the funds are withdrawn from your policy or borrowed against your policy, they DO NOT negatively affect the amount of taxes you have to pay on your Social Security benefits. This is a really big deal and can save you a boat-load of money. This is yet again, another reason that makes this the most powerful retirement program in America!

IULs Help You Avoid Probate

You can't really appreciate the value of this unless you've been involved in a lengthy and stressful probate battle in the past. They can get ugly and seem to drag on forever. Yet again, the IUL comes to the rescue. If you have an IUL, you can totally and completely avoid probate. Here's how it works.

When you set up your IUL, it is a life insurance contract. As part of setting it up, you name a beneficiary or beneficiaries and they become part of that contract. The laws are totally favorable to you again in this instance. When the policy holder passes away, the death benefit funds are paid DIRECTLY to the named beneficiary(s) within only a matter of days. These funds are completely exempt from probate and drawn out legal battles. This advantage saves you a ton of time, money, aggravation and stress.

Become Your Own Bank

When you see those gigantic skyscraper buildings owned by the mega banks, do you ever wonder how they got so much money to pay for it all? A good bit of their profits comes from the interest that you pay them on your home loan, car loan, credit cards, etc. There's huge money in collecting interest payments. Banks use fractional reserve lending to earn interest on money they have already lent out. Our strategy allows you to use a similar method and to earn gains on the same money twice.

How would you like to never have to borrow another cent from a bank again? How would you like to put all of those interest payments in your pockets, and not in the bank's pockets anymore? With this program, you can actually become your own bank, and borrow the money from yourself. It's true. Heck, you can even be your own bank president.

After your IUL is established and funded, you'll have your own source of funds to turn to. The next time you need to borrow money to buy a car, a boat, a plane, send your kids to college, invest in a business, expand your business, buy real estate, or just about anything you can think of, you can forget about having to go down to the bank, get on your knees, and beg for a loan. You won't have to stress-out about having to qualify for a loan. You won't have to worry about how your credit score is doing. You won't need to worry about proving income or putting up assets as collateral. None of that BS anymore!

Since you are your own banker, of course you need to act responsibly and make wise decisions about your money.

However, as you know, over time, various financial needs will always arise. When a financial need arises, you simply have a meeting with yourself, (the bank President), and decide if the purchase is a wise decision. If so, you simply approve the loan, and borrow it from your IUL. You can set up your own terms to pay back the loan if you wish. Depending on your situation, you could choose to never pay the loan back. You are in complete control.

Imagine all of the interest you could save over a life-time if you did not have to borrow money from others, and pay interest to them? Even though interest rates are super low at this time, we all know there will come a time again when they go through the roof. When that time comes, it will be very comforting to know you have your own source of funds to turn to.

CHAPTER 15

Creating A Lifetime Income

One of the most exciting parts of the IUL is the possibility for lifetime, tax-free income. Our clients absolutely love this! Here's why.

If you set up, structure, fund and manage your IU properly, your IUL can generate a tax-free retirement income for you that can pay you each and every year until you are 110 or 120 years old. We specialize in helping you set up, structure and manage your IUL for maximum success. That's what we do.

Imagine how wonderful it will feel to know that you have a lifetime, tax-free income that comes in each and every month during your retirement.

And, if something comes up, and you need a lump-sum of money; you just borrow it from your policy. There's no need to have to ask anyone for it, or qualify, or fill out a ton of paperwork, get on your knees and beg for it. It's your money, and you have access to it at any time you wish.

You can have a great peace-of-mind knowing your policy is managed and backed up by a 132 year-old company with a stellar track record. They only invest in the most conservative financial instruments and take very, very little risk. That's how they've managed to grow and thrive for over a century.

Want to see how your life-time income could look? We would be happy to run some scenarios for you.

How You Can Have 1 Million Dollars a Year, Tax-Free, For Life

How would you like to have a million dollar a year, tax-free retirement income for life? Okay, I know this doesn't apply to most people reading this book, but let's check it out real quick, just for fun.

Using our specialized version of the IUL, if a 45 year old put in $350,000 a year, for 7 years, and then never put in a single dime after that. When he retires at age 65, assuming average market returns, he would be able to pull a million dollars a year from his policy, completely tax-free, and he would be able to pull a million dollars out, each and every year, until he reached 110 years-old. *Pretty amazing, right!* Assuming the above performance, if he lived to age 84, he would have put 2.45 million into the policy and would have pulled 19 million out of it during his retirement.

If you're saying to yourself, that's amazing, but I don't have that kind of money to put into an IUL, just keep in mind that the investment amounts can vary, but the *power* of this program remains the same. The ratios are pretty much the same, so it does not matter if you are rich or not, the same growth factors apply.

We would be happy to run various illustrations for you that will clearly show you exactly how much money you could have each year, tax-free, in retirement. Most clients are very pleasantly surprised to find out how much of a life-time income they can have coming in each year during their retirement from their IUL.

CHAPTER 16

How Does the IUL Compare To a ROTH IRA

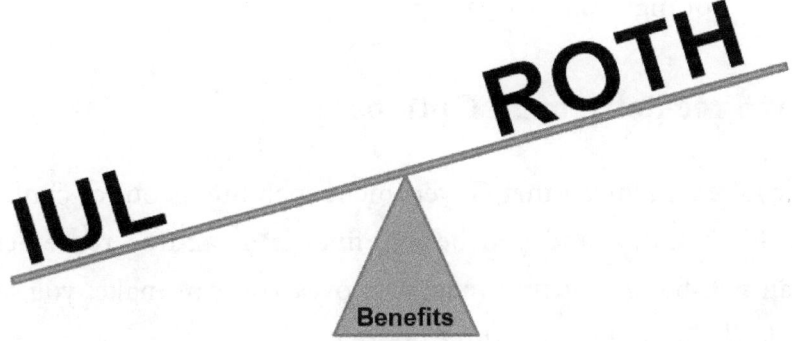

We get this question from time to time. Some people will say, *"This sounds just like my ROTH account, without the insurance. I fund my ROTH account with after taxed funds, my account grows over time, and I pay no taxes on the funds when I pull them out in retirement."* That's all true; however, there are some MAJOR differences between the two programs.

Here's a quick comparison: Currently, a ROTH IRA is the only traditional financial retirement vehicle that allows you to withdraw your money during retirement tax-free. However, the ROTH has two BIG LIMITATIONS:

(1) Annual contributions are capped at *approximately* $5,500 per year. (The tax code is much too long to give all the details about ROTH contributions here, but this amount will serve as a good general amount for this discussion.) So your contribution amounts are very limited. If you need to "make up lost ground" fast with your retirement program, this limitation is going to severely limit you.

(2) Here's another BIG problem with the ROTH. If you make more than *"approximately"* $191,000 a year, you are NOT ALLOWED to open a ROTH IRA. Boom. *Door slammed in your face!* The ROTH is simply not an option for high-income earners.

Tax-Free Retirement Options

If you're convinced that Government spending is out of control in this country, and you believe finding a tax-free retirement plan will be one of the smartest moves you can make, you are basically limited to only three options.

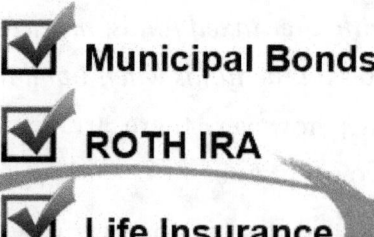

Municipal Bonds –

Income from municipal bonds is not subject to federal income tax and depending on which state you live in, may be exempt from state and local taxes. The problem with municipal bonds is that over time, they do not have high enough returns to make them suitable for most people's retirement funds, plus they only offer limited diversification.

ROTH IRA –

As stated above, if you are a high-income earner, or if you need to make up for lost ground with higher than allowed annual contributions, you are out of luck with a ROTH. Plus, you have to adhere to the ROTH withdrawal guidelines and have limited investment options.

Life Insurance –

Life Insurance is the hands-down clear winner here. Depending on your qualifications, there is NO LIMIT to the amount you can invest. So if you need to make up for lost ground, or if you want to sock away a ton of money for retirement, life insurance lets you do that. You can invest your funds in ANYTHING you wish and withdraw your funds at any time you wish with no penalties or fees.

So if you are looking for a smart way to invest larger sums of money into an account where you can withdraw it 100% tax-free, the IUL is the _ONLY_ real option.

As mentioned in the beginning of this book, that's why so many rich families, large companies and institutions are using this method so aggressively. They desperately want to protect and save every penny they can from taxes.

CHAPTER 17

Part 2:
Outside Investment Accelerator or (Double Dipping)

Now we're going to really get into the strategies that the ultra-rich have been using for centuries to massively grow their wealth. For the most part, these strategies have been largely unknown and unavailable to the average investor. Up until now, there's simply been few easy and affordable vehicles available for the average person to participate in this type of thing unless you had an army of attorneys and the best financial minds on the planet devising and implementing these types of multiplication strategies.

> **You have the option to earn returns on your funds from two (2) different areas, at the same time.**

Lucky for us, the Government has granted these amazing options as part of the specialized benefits of IUL policies. If you work with a skilled and specially trained advisor, and set up and fund your IUL policy correctly...

This is such a powerful program! When you fully understand how much of a difference it can make in your retirement program, you will lose some sleep thinking about it for sure.

Our clients are absolutely delighted with this option. It gives them diversification and outstanding peace of mind. They know their IUL retirement program has the potential to grow and grow with no market downside risk, while they invest those same funds into other areas.

Some clients are content to just stay with core part of the IUL program and not take advantage of the leveraging options the program offers. And that's perfectly fine. It's your choice.

Everyone has different needs and tolerances, and you should always do what you're comfortable with. However, if you're looking for a way to possibly put your retirement on steroids, *you're going to love Part 2.*

Often when clients first come to us, they plug their numbers into our custom Barefoot Retirement calculator that we give you and discover that they're not going to have near enough to retire the way they want to.

Their options are often limited to;

(a) Keep doing what they have been doing and make the decision to continue working during retirement.

(b) Decide to retire at a much lower standard of living than they had hoped to.

(c) Choose to utilize the power of leverage and put their retirement funds to work for them, on double duty, to potentially make up lost ground and still be able to reach their retirement goals.

We use a number of different names to describe the concept, but one of the main ones is:

The Power of Leverage

The Power of LEVERAGE is amazing! Now, you don't have to settle for either/or if you don't want to. This strategy gives you the power to employ 2 different investment options, with the same money, at the same time, and earn returns on **BOTH** of them. And before you ask, of course this is 100% legal, ethical, moral and doable.

First let me give you a simplified general idea of the strategy, then I'll break it down into detail of how it works within our strategy.

Let's just say you had $100,000, and you put it into our blended index fund. This concept allows you to keep the initial $100,000 working and earning for you, but allows you to borrow against it and invest the majority of those same funds into any type of investment you wish. *Any type!* And it gives you the potential to earn two different returns on the same money.

So if your investments perform well, you have the potential to earn two different returns on the SAME funds. Pretty amazing, right? Can you imagine how much faster your retirement funds could grow if you had them working for you in two different places at the same time?

Initial & Future Contributions　　　**Subsequent Investment**

Leveraged the initial contribution amount into other investments

Earn ___%　　　**AND**　　　Earn ___%

To put this in perspective, let's compare this to a regular IRA or 401k. Try calling up your broker and saying something like this, *"He Bill. You know the 100k I invested in my IRA? I want to take most of it out and invest it in something else, but I want to keep earning the standard returns you get for me on the 100k in my IRA. That's okay, right? I mean, you can do that for me, right?"* Just try that and see what happens.

Now, let's break this down and see exactly how this works.

First off, it's important to know that a life insurance policy is by definition tax-deferred, it's not tax-free. The cash value of an IUL policy grows without being taxed. However, IF the money is **"withdrawn,"** then all the gains within the policy (the amount earned in addition to the total premiums paid) will be taxed as income and not as capital gains. Rest assured that our strategy does not involve 'withdrawing' your funds nor having to pay taxes on them.

Our method gives you **Tax-Free Access to your funds**. The key is doing it correctly, and that's why it is so important to work with people who are specifically skilled on these exact types of policies like our team is.

Our clients use a contractual policy feature that allows a policy holder to have access to tax-free money in their policy by using their life insurance cash value as collateral. It's called a Policy Loan Provision and is one of the most valuable and amazing aspects of this program. When executed correctly, the policy owner is able to avoid any and ALL taxes on the funds they receive. The distinction here is that it is simply a loan from a financial institution and NOT a withdrawal from an insurance policy.

(Note, a policy holder is able to take a tax-free withdrawal from their policy only up to the amount of total premiums paid into the policy to date, subject to surrender charges, because those funds were taxed before they went into the policy. If you choose to withdraw funds above the total premiums paid, the withdrawal of the gain is taxed as income. When using our strategy correctly, you will not be withdrawing funds.)

When you use the policy loan provision correctly, as we advise you, you take out a loan AGAINST the cash value in the policy. You are not taking out a loan FROM the cash value and there is a huge difference here. The cash value within the policy is the collateral for the loan.

Remember when you borrowed money to buy your last car? Was the loan that you got from the bank taxed? No. Loans are not taxed. Yes, you probably paid tax on the car when you bought it but the loan itself was not taxed. The distinction here is that loans are not taxed. When you buy goods and services, they are taxed, but not loans.

Also, when you borrow money in the form of a loan, you have to pay interest on the loan, right? Correct. That's true. When setting up your IUL and structuring policy loans, there are quite a few different options available and your advisor will give you great advice in this area. At the time this book is being written, the average amount charged for policy loans by the issuing insurance company is around 4.5%.

So how and when do we pay the cost of funds back?

As you may have guessed by now, there are lots of different options here.

Option 1: You NEVER have to pay it back during your lifetime. That's right? If you don't pay the interest back the insurance company will simply deduct it from your death benefit amount. They policy should still be monitored carefully each year to ensure the ratios are fine, but as long as you do this correctly, you can take out a loan against your policy and never, ever have to pay it back if you don't wish to. I'll show you an example of how this works in just a moment.

Option 2: You can pay back as much as you wish, when you wish. You have total flexibility here. You get to choose if you want to pay back the interest charges and if so, how much you want to pay back and when you want to pay them back. (Don't you wish your bank was this easy to work with?)

Option 3: Wash Loan Provision. One of your options is to choose a fixed indexed return on the cash value of your account. Currently, the fixed return is around 3.5%. These amounts do vary from time to time but generally speaking, if it cost you 4.5% to borrow the funds, and if you can choose to receive a 3.5% fixed return, then the net cost of your loan is only about 1%. Plus, with our flagship product, after 10 years the company drops the wash loan amount down to .1%.

While most people borrow the funds against their policies from the insurance company itself, you always have the option to go to any outside institution and borrow the funds from them. Some of our clients are doing this right now and are borrowing from banks at rates around 2% to 3%. Why you may ask would a bank give a borrower such a low rate? It's because the loan is collateralized by the cash value of the life insurance policy, and that's one of the most secure forms of collateral a lender can have. Note, getting a loan from a bank is not guaranteed and may require a lot more effort than just calling the insurance company.

How Long Do You Have To Wait To Borrow Funds From Your Policy?

Most similar policies and most Whole Life policies require that you wait many years before you can begin to borrow funds from your policy.

However, some of our clients choose to purchase a rider on their policy that enables them to borrow up to approximately 80% of the cash value of their policy beginning in the very first month that your policy is taken out. This can be a huge benefit. (Note: There are lots of options when setting up these policies so the percentage amount that can be borrowed can vary depending on many variables.)

The great news is that since the funds are distributed as a loan, they DO NOT show up in any tax reporting, and they will NOT be shown on your tax returns.

Hence, it's PRIVATE!

For most of the people I know and talk with, privacy is a huge issue these days. The more they can stay off the grid, the better!

This is Tax-Free money that you can use throughout your life, and the IRS can't touch a penny of it.

It's important to note that you shouldn't take too much money out of your policy to the point that the policy becomes non self-sustaining. Again, this is where your advisor can help keep your policy safeguarded and functioning correctly. It's not hard to do at all, but you should just be aware of it and monitor it from time to time.

What Does My Policy Look Like If I Never Pay My Loans Back?

Some people initially have a hard time wrapping their mind around this concept. It just doesn't seem plausible that you can borrow the money from your policy, not pay a single penny back, and still have your policy give you a great lifetime, tax-free income... Plus have the money you borrowed out of it to boot. Right? Well, I totally understand that. I'll prove it to you right now with an actual IUL illustration.

In this illustration below we took a 48-year-old man whom we will call Don and structured the policy where he would invest $100,000 per year, each year, for 7 years. After the 7th year, Don would NEVER have to put another penny into the policy, ever.

(If you happen not to be a high-income earner or don't have a larger amount to invest, please don't let the $100,000 example scare you. It's an easy round number to demonstrate this with. If you only have several hundred dollars a month to put into a policy, you can still participate and still get **ALL** of the awesome benefits of this program.)

Without getting into all of the details of the illustration below, let's just focus on a few main points.

A. In the red box area where you see the **A**, that shows where the policy holder invests $100,000 per year for 7 years. That was his premium outlay amount.

B. In the red box area where you see the **C**, that shows where the policy holder borrowed $80,000 a year from his policy, each year, for 7 years. Over 7 years Don borrows $560,000 from the policy. (More detail on this in a moment. We can also structure policies where you can borrow over 90% however, we wanted to keep this example somewhat conservative.)

C. In the red box area where you see the **B**, that shows where the policy holder, at age 65 starts borrowing $120,000 of tax-free money, each and every year, until he dies or until he reaches 120 years old.

Year	Age	Premium Outlay	Partial Surrender	Policy Loan	Loan Interest	Net Outlay	Accumulation Value	Surrender Value	Death Benefit^
1	48	100,000	0	81,650	1,650	20,000	92,200	10,218	1,946,988
2	49	100,000	0	85,900	5,900	20,000	191,370	23,138	1,959,908
3	50	100,000	0	90,195	10,195	20,000	298,005	39,211	1,975,981
4	51	100,000	0	94,704	14,704	20,000	412,661	58,776	1,995,546
5	52	100,000	0	99,440	19,440	20,000	535,901	82,172	2,018,942
6	53	100,000	0	104,412	24,412	20,000	668,377	109,811	2,046,581
7	54	100,000	0	109,632	29,632	20,000	810,755	142,109	2,078,880 #
8	55	0	0	33,297	33,297	0	864,125	162,048	823,101
9	56	0	0	34,961	34,961	0	921,636	184,455	787,997
10	57	0	0	36,710	36,710	0	983,566	209,526	751,138
11	58	0	0	38,545	38,545	0	1,066,046	253,303	712,436
12	59	0	0	40,472	40,472	0	1,156,199	302,819	695,926
13	60	0	0	42,496	42,496	0	1,254,339	358,291	734,592
14	61	0	0	44,621	44,621	0	1,361,035	420,184	801,274
15	62	0	0	46,852	46,852	0	1,476,965	489,071	873,082
16	63	0	0	49,194	49,194	0	1,602,861	565,573	950,259
17	64	0	0	51,654	51,654	0	1,739,515	650,362	1,033,055
18	65	0	0	176,962	56,962	-120,000	1,887,782	620,946	998,503
19	66	0	0	185,811	65,811	-120,000	2,048,663	595,260	984,506
20	67	0	0	195,101	75,101	-120,000	2,223,242	573,942	974,126
21	68	0	0	204,856	84,856	-120,000	2,412,697	557,707	967,865
22	69	0	0	215,099	95,099	-120,000	2,618,301	547,335	966,263
23	70	0	0	225,854	105,854	-120,000	2,841,430	543,691	969,905
24	71	0	0	237,147	117,147	-120,000	3,083,580	547,727	948,593
25	72	0	0	249,004	129,004	-120,000	3,346,371	560,500	928,601

Year	Age	Premium Outlay	Partial Surrender	Policy Loan	Loan Interest	Net Outlay	Accumulation Value	Surrender Value	Death Benefit^
26	73	0	0	261,454	141,454	-120,000	3,631,563	583,173	910,014
27	74	0	0	274,527	154,527	-120,000	3,941,067	617,031	892,906
28	75	0	0	288,253	168,253	-120,000	4,276,953	663,491	877,338
29	76	0	0	302,666	182,666	-120,000	4,641,472	724,110	956,184
30	77	0	0	317,799	197,799	-120,000	5,037,064	800,608	1,052,461
31	78	0	0	333,689	213,689	-120,000	5,466,377	894,873	1,168,192
32	79	0	0	350,374	230,374	-120,000	5,932,286	1,008,981	1,305,595
33	80	0	0	367,892	247,892	-120,000	6,437,911	1,145,215	1,467,111
34	81	0	0	386,287	266,287	-120,000	6,986,638	1,306,081	1,655,413
35	82	0	0	405,601	285,601	-120,000	7,582,139	1,494,329	1,873,436
36	83	0	0	425,881	305,881	-120,000	8,228,403	1,712,976	2,124,397
37	84	0	0	447,175	327,175	-120,000	8,929,757	1,965,333	2,411,821
38	85	0	0	469,534	349,534	-120,000	9,690,896	2,255,026	2,739,570
39	86	0	0	493,011	373,011	-120,000	10,516,918	2,586,028	3,111,874
40	87	0	0	517,661	397,661	-120,000	11,413,353	2,962,692	3,533,360
41	88	0	0	543,544	423,544	-120,000	12,386,202	3,389,783	4,009,093
42	89	0	0	570,722	450,722	-120,000	13,441,981	3,872,515	4,544,614
43	90	0	0	599,258	479,258	-120,000	14,587,758	4,416,593	5,145,981
44	91	0	0	629,221	509,221	-120,000	15,831,205	5,028,256	5,661,504
45	92	0	0	660,682	540,682	-120,000	17,180,647	5,714,325	6,229,744
46	93	0	0	693,716	573,716	-120,000	18,644,463	6,481,598	6,854,488
47	94	0	0	728,401	608,401	-120,000	20,226,983	7,332,749	7,535,019
48	95	0	0	764,821	644,821	-120,000	21,951,169	8,288,999	8,288,999
49	96	0	0	803,063	683,063	-120,000	23,822,329	9,353,824	9,353,824
50	97	0	0	843,216	723,216	-120,000	25,852,989	10,537,833	10,537,833
51	98	0	0	885,376	765,376	-120,000	28,056,747	11,852,607	11,852,607
52	99	0	0	929,645	809,645	-120,000	30,448,357	13,310,785	13,310,785
53	100	0	0	976,128	856,128	-120,000	33,043,832	14,926,155	14,926,155
54	101	0	0	1,024,934	904,934	-120,000	35,860,550	16,713,764	16,713,764
55	102	0	0	1,076,181	956,181	-120,000	38,917,371	18,690,020	18,690,020
56	103	0	0	1,129,990	1,009,990	-120,000	42,234,761	20,872,816	20,872,816
57	104	0	0	1,186,489	1,066,489	-120,000	45,834,931	23,281,664	23,281,664
58	105	0	0	1,245,814	1,125,814	-120,000	49,741,993	25,937,836	25,937,836
59	106	0	0	1,308,104	1,188,104	-120,000	53,982,105	28,864,515	28,864,515
60	107	0	0	1,373,509	1,253,509	-120,000	58,583,660	32,086,964	32,086,964
61	108	0	0	1,442,185	1,322,185	-120,000	63,577,466	35,632,710	35,632,710
62	109	0	0	1,514,294	1,394,294	-120,000	68,996,962	39,531,742	39,531,742
63	110	0	0	1,590,009	1,470,009	-120,000	74,878,434	43,816,727	43,816,727
64	111	0	0	1,669,509	1,549,509	-120,000	81,261,262	48,523,244	48,523,244
65	112	0	0	1,752,985	1,632,985	-120,000	88,188,184	53,690,040	53,690,040
66	113	0	0	1,840,634	1,720,634	-120,000	95,705,581	59,359,304	59,359,304
67	114	0	0	1,932,666	1,812,666	-120,000	103,863,786	65,576,969	65,576,969
68	115	0	0	2,029,299	1,909,299	-120,000	112,717,424	72,393,041	72,393,041
69	116	0	0	2,130,764	2,010,764	-120,000	122,325,777	79,861,948	79,861,948
70	117	0	0	2,237,302	2,117,302	-120,000	132,753,178	88,042,932	88,042,932
71	118	0	0	2,349,167	2,229,167	-120,000	144,069,446	97,000,462	97,000,462
72	119	0	0	2,466,626	2,346,626	-120,000	156,350,351	106,804,691	106,804,691
73	120	0	0	2,589,957	2,469,957	-120,000	169,678,121	117,531,954	117,531,954
Total:		700,000	0	51,934,580	44,654,580	-6,580,000			

It's that absolutely amazing!

Here the policy holder borrows $80,000 a year for each of the 7 years. He can choose to borrow nothing, or chose to borrow any amount he wishes per year, up to the $80,000 amount shown in this illustration. He can take that $80,000 a year and invest it in ANYTHING he wants to. He does not have to ask anyone for permission, and he does not have to abide by any guidelines that dictate where he can put the money.

This is your retirement fund so it is serious business, and you should only invest these funds into solid and safe investments that you believe will serve you the best. But just to be crystal clear and to make a point, if you want to borrow those funds and take a vacation around the world, you could. You could choose to spend it all on a new home or boat, plane, on medical costs, give it to charity, or buy anything your heart desires. The point is, *YOU get to choose.* Neither the Government nor any other entity is there to tell you what you can and cannot do with your money.

Hopefully, the policy holder will choose wisely and make wise investments that will help fund the retirement of his dreams. If he makes some wise investment decisions, he could turn that $560,000 into millions, by the time he retires.

Here is the great part. It doesn't matter if he makes millions with the funds borrowed, or if he lost it all on a wild weekend in Las Vegas. As long as the policy continues to perform as illustrated above, when he turns age 65, he will get to take $120,000 of tax-free income out per year, each and every year, until he either dies or reaches age 120. How powerful is that? Imagine the peace-of-mind you could have with a safety-net like this?

By the way, if the policy holder happened to be in a 38% tax bracket when he started taking out the funds, the $120,000 tax-free dollars a year would be approximately the equivalent of $210,000 taxable dollars.

Lastly, the illustration above shows how the policy performs if he chooses to never pay back a single penny of the funds he borrowed. If he did choose to pay back some or all of the borrowed funds, the more he pays back, the larger the Net Outlay is or the amount of tax-free dollars that he gets to take out during retirement, each and every year until he dies or reaches 120 years old.

In the example above, if Don paid back the loans he borrowed each year, his net outlay would increase to approximately $240,000 per year until he reaches 120 years old.

What Investment Options Do You Have With the Funds You Borrow?

That's always a great question that comes up. The reason it comes up so frequently is because most people are so *"conditioned"* by the rules, regulations and restrictions of qualified retirement plans like IRAs, 401(k), etc., they are just accustomed to having strict limitation's dictating what you can invest in and what you can't invest in.

This is totally different.

With a properly structured IUL, you can invest in ANYTHING you want. Anything! There are no limitations what-so-ever. You can keep your IUL locked up, in the blended index account, earning 0% to 17% a year, with zero chance of losing a penny due to market downturns, and then take out a loan against your policy and invest it in anything you wish.

Here is a short list of just some of the things you can invest in:

- ☐ Businesses, business equipment, sustaining and growing your business, business loans, etc.
- ☐ Real Estate of any type, notes and mortgages
- ☐ Precious Metals of any type (gold, silver, platinum, palladium, etc.)
- ☐ Oil & Gas
- ☐ Stocks, Bonds, Mutual Funds, ETFs, etc.
- ☐ Art & Collectibles of any type
- ☐ Cars, boats, airplanes, etc. (It's usually better to choose assets that are likely to increase in value.)

With this program, you can invest in anything that makes sense to you, that you believe you can make a positive return on, and that you believe is wise and safe.

CHAPTER 18

Maximizing The Barefoot Retirement Program

Like we said above, this strategy is not for everyone. Some people are content to just stay with all the amazing benefits of the IUL explained in Option 1, and that's perfectly fine.

However, if you are interested in really maximizing your returns, you've never seen anything else like this that's available for the average investor. Let's use the example of Bucket A and B below to explain how this works.

Bucket "A"

IUL Indexed Fund
0% to 17% Growth
Per Year

Bucket "B"

Optional Outside Investment
__% Growth Per Year

In this example, the investor purchases an IUL, selects the blended index account, purchases a rider to be able to borrow against his cash value within the first month, and puts $100,000 into the policy the first year. This is bucket A. (Again, we are using an example of $100,000 because it is an easy, round number, but you can invest just about any amount you wish.)

At the end of the year, the policy holder earns the actual blended indexed rate of return on his cash value amount. So if the market index goes down 18%, the gain is 0% and the cash value of the policy remains intact, and you have zero losses against your cash value due to market downturns.

On the other hand, if the market index goes up 23%, the policy holder will be credited with a 17% gain on the total cash value of his policy. (Note: There is an upside market cap of 17% and a market downside floor of 0 %.)

During the first month of the policy, since the policy holder purchased the rider, he can choose to borrow the majority of the cash value out of the policy. Let's just say he borrows $80,000 from bucket A. He takes the borrowed funds from bucket A and puts them in an alternative investment in bucket B.

Yes, he is currently being charged approximately 4.5% on the funds borrowed. However, he can choose to never pay the interest charges back at all, or pay them back in any amount at any time. It's totally up to him.

Now, let's just say, for example, that the policy holder takes the funds he borrowed from bucket A and invests them into an investment in bucket B where he earns 12%. Here's the amazing part. The policy holder continues to make the market returns on the funds in bucket A while at the same time earning the 12% (in our example) on those same funds (borrowed) and now in bucket B.

Keep in mind that if your Bucket B investment goes down, your returns for Bucket B go down. However, the amount you can earn on your Bucket B investments is unlimited. If you can find investments that return 20%, 30% or more per year, on funds that you "borrowed" from your policy (Bucket A), then your overall returns can be substantial.

Let's don't forget about the death benefit. The amount of the death benefit varies during the lifetime of the policy. Based on the illustration above, in the early years the death benefit is about 2 million dollars. I always like to compare the difference of putting funds into our program, to just putting the money into an IRA or a 401(k).

At the end of year one, with the IUL you have been able to leverage the values of your funds and have the potential to make an above-average total return on your funds, plus you have approximately a 2 million-dollar death benefit for your family to boot.

Compare this to just putting 100k into a 401(k).

(A) You only get to earn once on your money. You can't leverage it.

(B) You get zero death benefit.

(C) You will have to pay taxes on <u>all</u> of your funds when you pull them out.

I told you this program was powerful. Do you think returns like this could help you make up for lost ground in your retirement program? Do you think this could raise your horizons as to what could be possible with your retirement? Do you think this could help you to live the Barefoot Retirement lifestyle you've dreamed of?

Unlimited Investment Options
So What Can I Invest My Bucket B Funds In?

That's one of the biggest questions we were hearing from clients. They love this program. Most love the leverage option and really want to maximize their returns by double dipping and borrowing from bucket A, and investing those funds into bucket B.

The only problem is, most people don't know what to invest their bucket B funds into.

The average investor simply doesn't have a clue about what to invest in, nor the connections to find solid investments. We've all been killed by the stock market, and many of us suffered greatly with the housing market crash. Many of us are understandably gun-shy when it comes to investments. So how/where does the average investor know what to invest in?

It's always good to invest in what you know. If you are really good at something, completely understand it, and there's a way to invest in it, then that may be perfect for you. If you know real estate really well, are good at it, and know your local market, you could use the funds to invest in residential or commercial real estate.

If you own your own business, this program is the *PERFECT* solution for expanding and growing your business. You can read more on this concept in the Chapter below titled **The Barefoot Business Program**.

If the above options don't apply to you, or if you are looking for a *"hands-free"* investment that does not require time, hassles and effort to manage the investment, we may be able to introduce you to some great options.

Our Barefoot Retirement team has been in this industry for a quite a while. After years of experience, we've seen a lot of really bad investment options out there, that you should avoid like the plague. However, after sorting through tons of them, and through our connections, we've discovered a hand-full of options that we've found to be top-notch.

We always look for smart and ethical people, who've consistently delivered above-average returns. Additionally, we look for programs that have a very high percentage of their investors who continue to invest with them over, and over and over. That statistic alone, speaks volumes. Many of our Barefoot Retirement team members personally invest in many of these options as well. If you have an interest in finding out more about any of these programs, just ask us. We do not actively promote them. *You have to ask.*

We at the Barefoot Retirement group are not investment advisors, nor are we licensed securities dealers. You should ALWAYS seek the advice of a knowledgeable investment advisor and conduct your own due-diligence before making any investment decisions. We cannot, and do not, guarantee any specific results or returns with any of these options. As with any investment, it is possible to under-perform or lose money. Market conditions as well as results, can and do vary.

Regarding the investment options below, the Barefoot Retirement group does not own or manage these programs. If a client is interested in finding out more about any of these programs, and asks us for this information, we've been pre-approved to introduce potential investors to these closely held, and sometimes private programs.

Let me give you a brief overview of just some of the invest options that we've found to be excellent. (Some of these options, not all, but some of these, are strictly available 'by invitation only'.)

Real Estate –

We have a number of different Real Estate programs that we refer clients to. Remember the guy I told you about earlier in the book? The guy with the private investment group that has not had a single losing deal in over 19 years? Many clients choose to put some of their funds with him. In most of the deals he does, he actually gives you the title to your prorated share of the investment. His company handles 100% of everything so you don't need to get involved at all. Don't worry, no tenant is ever going to call you in the middle of the night when their toilet is stopped up.

By the way, he will not allow us to even mention the rates of returns that he routinely achieves for clients. Returns vary from deal to deal and are presented with each deal's offering. He always tries to under promise and over deliver. All I can say is the fact that 97% of his investors are repeat investors should give you an idea of how happy they are with the returns they are getting. Also, since he is a total value investor, when market conditions are not right for buying real estate, he does not buy. He is happy to sit on the sidelines for as long as it takes for the market to come around for him. He is conservative and VERY selective. That discipline is what enables him to be so successful.

Another Real Estate program that we refer clients to has an outstanding track record as well. They have been in business for over ten years and during the past 10-year period, they have averaged an 18% return for investors. During that time, they have had 3 deals that broke even, but the clients did not lose money. Over the past 10 years not one of their investors has lost a penny. Again, the track record speaks for itself. They average a 95% investor retention rate. In other words, 95% of the people who invest with them once, continue to invest with them in future investment deals, over and over.

As you know, past results are no guarantees of future returns, but that's a pretty impressive track record. Especially if these were your Bucket B returns, that you were getting in addition to your Bucket A returns.

Debt Deals –

This may seem strange to you if you've never heard of this before. This team is made up of experts in investing high-quality debt. It's been tested and tweaked for years. Offices are spread out around the world and the systems they use are cutting edge, state of the art.

They typically do these deals with some of the wealthiest families in the world. Family names who are house-hold, recognizable names. These guys know how to make money and rarely lose money. Return rates are typically in the 12% range, but the returns are not guaranteed. There's always risk in any investment deals but the beauty of working with these guys is that you get to invest at the same level, and use the same systems that the largest and smartest guys in the world are using.

Collateral Loan Deals --

At the time of writing this book, a Patent is being submitted for this program, so we can't give you any detailed information without first signing an NDA (Non-disclosure agreement.) What I can tell you is this is an investment loan deal that typically pays out around 10% to 12%, and it's completely backed by some of the safest and most solid types of collateralized loans available. When most investors discover the details on how this works, their only question is, "How much can I put in?"

The beauty of the Barefoot Retirement program is you can choose to invest in anything you wish. You can also move in and out of investments as you wish. If you believe gold and silver are ready to break-out to a big move upwards, you can buy precious metals. If you come across a great deal on a rental unit or apartment building that you know will be a great revenue generator for you, you can invest in that. It's your money, and you can invest it *ANY* way you wish.

This vehicle gives you the ability to double-dip and gives you the possibility to earn two different returns on the <u>same</u> money.

Taxes For Buckets A and B

Bucket A: It's important to be aware of this. As stated earlier, when you begin to take funds out of your bucket A, typically during retirement, if you take them out in the form of a loan against the cash value of your policy as we advise, they will be 100% completely tax free. Your policy can be structured so that you never have to pay back the loans or the interest charges for the loans if you don't want to.

Here's a simplistic example to help explain the concept. Let's say you reach the age when you want to finally retire and start living off of the funds you've built up in your IUL cash value account. Let's say the cash value is 1 million dollars, and you start pulling out $150,000 to live on each year.

The beauty of this program is that since you *"borrow"* the $150,000 from your account each year, you still have the full 1 million dollars of cash value working for you each year. Your cash value account has the possibility to continue to grow and build, (depending on the market index performance). This makes it possible that you would never run out of money. Plus the $150,000 you take out each year is completely tax-free.

Let's say in this example you live until the age 95. You have 1.5 million in loans against your policy. Your death benefit at the time of death is 2.5 million. When you die, the insurance company takes the 1.5 million from your death benefit, and pays off the loans against your policy.

That leaves 1 million dollars which the insurance company gives to your beneficiaries. That 1 million dollars is tax-free to them. So to recap; you never had to pay your policy loans or loan interest back. You got to enjoy the money you took out in the form of tax-free loans, and your beneficiaries got a tax-free winfall to boot. Not too bad, wouldn't you say?

Bucket B: It's important to know that all of your gains from bucket B are taxable, so you will need to account for that. If you structure it correctly, bucket A proceeds are NOT taxable but the gains from bucket B are taxable as ordinary gains. Some people look at the gains from bucket B as kind of *"found"* money that they would not have had otherwise, and are happy to taxes on this money.

CHAPTER 19

The Barefoot Retirement Calculator

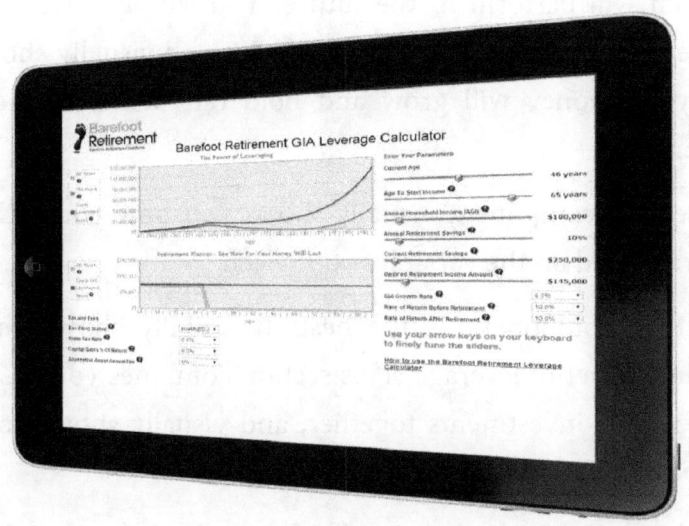

Putting It All Together -- The Real Power Of Leverage

We realize that some of these concepts and programs can be a little hard to understand in the beginning. There are quite a few moving parts and variables, and if you are new to this, it can sometimes be a challenge. To help our clients understand and visualize this better, we created a customized Barefoot Retirement Calculator.

There's no other calculator in the world like this one. Its custom made and one-of-a-kind. I have to tell you, our clients absolutely love it! *Caution: This calculator can become addicting.*

The Barefoot Retirement Calculator is super easy to use, and it gives you an excellent visual representation of the programs you are considering. There are three core components to it.

The first component is for seeing how your current retirement program will perform in the future. You simply plug in some simple numbers and assumptions, and it will visually show you how your money will grow and hold out before and during retirement.

The second component visually shows you how your IUL can perform based on the variables you select.

The third component is the best! It visually shows you the amazing power of leverage. This section combines your IUL and your outside investments together, and visually shows you just how powerful this combination can be.

To help you better understand how it works, let's take a look at two different examples.

Example 1:

In this example, we have a 46-year-old who makes $100,000 a year. He has accumulated $250,000 in his portfolio, and puts this amount into an IUL. *That's it.* He makes NO further contributions to his policy. He retires at age 65, and is then able to borrow $125,000 a year from his account, each and every single year, until age 120.

Wow. He was only making 100k a year while he was working. Now by only putting in 250k, he will be able to have a higher annual income during retirement, than he did while working. Plus... the 100k he made while working was taxable. The $125,000 a year he borrows from his policy each year is TAX-FREE. If he was in the 28% tax bracket while working, he was only netting out around $72,000 a year.

Who says that you have to downsize your lifestyle when you retire? That's what the Barefoot Retirement Plan is all about.

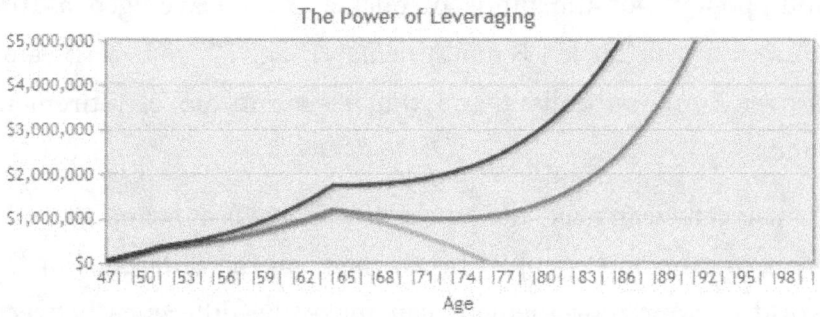

Red Line: The red line (GIA Asset), shows what your gains would have been if you **ONLY** invested in the **IUL**, the market index returns for the IUL averaged a 9% overall gain, over the years shown; you did not borrow against your policy, and you did not make any alternative investments into bucket B. You can see around age 77; the cash value of this account is over 1 million dollars, and you never run out of retirement funds.

Green Line: The green line (Alternative asset), shows what your gains would have been if you had **ONLY** invested in an alternative investment that averaged a 10% return over the years shown. The alternative investment could represent your IRA, 401(k) or any other investment you would have made. On this chart, you can see that the green line **crashes below zero** around age 77. That means, if that's your only retirement income, you are now 77 years old and out of money. *Ouch!* Can you say, "Welcome to....?"

Blue Line: The blue line (Combined Leverage asset), shows the power of leverage. It shows what the total value of your account would be if you put 250k into an IUL, and then made no further contributions to your policy, **AND** you borrowed a loan against your policy, put the funds in bucket B, and averaged a 10% return on your bucket B investments. At age 77, your cash value is over 2 million dollars, and you *never* run out of retirement funds.

As you can clearly see, the power of leverage is amazing and life-changing for most people. It can make all the difference in the world to your retirement. It can make the difference between you being able to live the barefoot retirement lifestyle of your dreams, or having to work into your golden years, just to survive.

Example 2:

In this example, we have a 40 year-old, who makes $75,000 a year. He does a good job managing his money, and manages to save approximately 13% of his gross income, or $833 a month, which he puts into his IUL each month. We are using a 9% return on his IUL, which has been the historical average for over 24 years. Plus, he borrows against his policy and achieves a 10% return per year, in outside investments, (in his bucket B).

He decides to retire at 65 years of age. When he retires, he will be able to borrow a retirement income out of his policy of $125,000 a year, for the rest of his life! Again, it's pretty amazing that someone who only made 75k a year while working, can achieve a lifetime retirement income of 125k a year, for life.

Plus, remember, the 125k per year is tax-free money. He gets to keep it ALL, and give none of it to Uncle Sam. He is making **67% MORE** in retirement, than he was making while working.

Now, to make this even more interesting, let's take a look at the lines on the chart below.

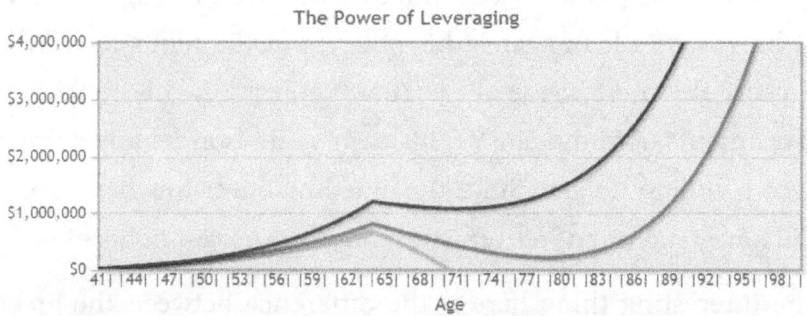

Red Line: The red line (GIA Asset), shows what his gains would have been if he **ONLY** invested in the **IUL**, the market index returns for the IUL averaged a 9% overall gain, over the years shown; if he did <u>NOT</u> borrow against your policy, and he did not make any alternative investments into bucket B. You can see, around age 80, is the low point. The cash value of his account at this low point is only around $200,000. However, here is the key takeaway. **The red line never touches zero.** That means he NEVER runs out of money during retirement. If he lives to 90, his cash value goes up to about 1.3 million.

Green Line: The green line (Alternative asset), shows what his gains would have been if he had **ONLY** invested in an alternative investment that averaged a 10% return over the years shown. The alternative investment could represent his IRA, 401(k) or any other investment he would have made. On this chart, you can see that the green line *crashes below zero* around age 71. That means, if this is his only source of retirement income, he is completely and out of money, at the *no-so-old* age of 71. Then what? Unfortunately, there are no good options at this point.

Blue Line: The blue line (Combined Leverage asset), shows the power of leverage. It shows what the total value of his account would be if he put $833 a month into his IUL until age 65. **AND** he borrowed a loan against his policy, put the funds to work in bucket B, and averaged a 10% return on his bucket B investments. Around age 71, his cash value is at its low point of over 1 million dollars. Since the blue line never touches zero, he will *never* run out of retirement funds, for the rest of his life.

The interesting thing here is the difference between the green, and blue line at age 71. By not using this program, he is out of money, and flat busted at the age of 71. However, if he follows the Barefoot Retirement Plan, (and if our return assumptions at least meet the return percentages we used for this analysis), instead of being broke at age 71, he would have a cash value net worth of over a million dollars, and a $125,000 annual, tax-free income, for as long as he lives. Talk about two different lifestyles, this is a pretty huge difference.

Some of you reading this may not have $833 a month to put into an IUL. Here's the thing. What if you cut this in half? What if you only put in half as much, and if you only received half as much in retirement? That's still pretty amazing. Or, what if you had two or three times more, to put into your IUL. Imagine what your retirement numbers would look like? Well, you don't have to imagine. We'll be happy to run those numbers for you for free. Just contact us and request your free analysis, and we will be happy to show it to you in vivid detail.

The two main variables in these examples are the percentage of return that the blended index will deliver in the years to come, and the percentage of return you can achieve with your outside investments in your bucket B. The blended index we most often use, has averaged a 9.24% return over the last 24 years. As you know, those have been some pretty crazy years. How will it perform in the next 25 or so years? No one knows. If it performs better, you plan will do better. If it performs worse, your plan will not perform as well. There are no guarantees of what the future holds, nor how the markets perform.

Additionally, no one knows how your outside investments will perform. You could have a low performance with your investment choices, or you could even lose all of your money. If that happens, your plan obviously would not perform as well. On the other hand, it's possible that you could make some excellent investment choices that have outstanding returns. This would cause your plan to perform even better.

If you find that these risks are more than you would be comfortable with, perhaps this program is not for you. It's not for everybody.

Fourth Quarter Playbook

The majority of Americans are not even close to being financially prepared for retirement. They are so far behind where they need to be; it's depressing. If they keep doing what they've been doing, and keep getting the same results they've been getting, it's a mathematical certainty that they will not reach their retirement goals, and will not have enough funds to retire the way they plan to.

Here's a great analogy for this. You're sitting in your favorite chair, in your den, watching your favorite football team, play on a Sunday afternoon. They just reached the fourth quarter. Your team is behind by 27 points. *Yikes.* The coach has been calling running plays, for most of the day. They obviously haven't been working so hot, against this dominant defense. You know the feeling you get, as you are screaming at the TV.

You know that if that coach doesn't do something different, if he doesn't change up his game-plan and playbook, if he doesn't start calling some down-the-field passing plays, they're going to lose this game. The clock is going to run out on them, they won't have enough time to make up the 27 points, and they're going to chalk up another loss on the season. You scream louder at the coach, saying something like this, *"Come on man. Call some passing plays. We can win this one. Let's get it going. Throw the damn ball, and let's score some touchdowns...."*

Some people are in a similar spot with their retirement. The clock is ticking down. There's not much time left. If you're going to get it done, and win the retirement game, you're going to have to do something different. You certainly don't want to panic, and throw caution to the wind. You don't want to throw *Hail-Mary* passes on every play. You need to be smart about it. But you also need to remember Einstein's famous quote, *"Insanity is doing the same thing over and over again, and expecting different results."*

Of all of the retirement programs out there that we've ever seen, we've never seen one as powerful as this. Not even close. As you can see by running different scenarios on your Barefoot Retirement Calculator, this program does have the potential to help you make up for lost ground, win the game, and be able to retire on your own terms. However, just like the coach has no guarantees that if he changes his play calling, that he'll win the game, neither do we. If the markets don't perform, or if we make some bad decisions along the way, they could affect our outcome.

On the other hand, the coach probably knows, or should know, that if he keeps playing-it-safe, and calling those same running plays that haven't worked all day, that he will lose the game. As we have said all along, retirement planning is serious business, and it should be given a great deal of thought.

We want to give you a FREE GIFT.

We want to give you our custom built Barefoot Retirement Calculator. We've spent many months as well as thousands of dollars developing this tool. We want to give it to you as our gift to you, simply for taking the time to check out the Barefoot Retirement Program.

It will help you take an in-depth look at what your retirement looks like now… and what it could look like using this amazing program. It will also demonstrate the Power of LEVERAGE. You'll be able to plug in your own numbers, your own investment amounts, your years until retirement and your own investment return assumptions. We think you'll love it. It's fun to run all kinds of *"What If"* scenarios. You'll find it to be an eye-opener.

To Gain FREE ACCESS To Your Barefoot Retirement Calculator, Go To: www.BarefootRetirement.com/calculator

Grab Your Free Calculator Now!

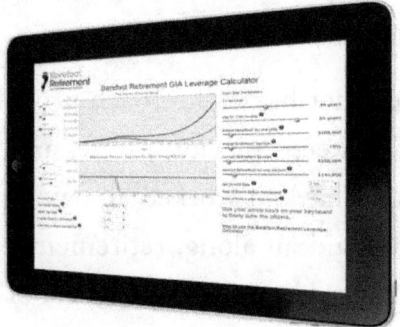

CHAPTER 20

Barefoot Business Owners Program

If you're a business owner, you're going to *love* this chapter.

Most business owners are independent thinkers. They're hardworking, risk taking, tax paying employers, and they are the backbone of this great country we are blessed to live in. It seems like there's hardly a day that goes by where the Government or some regulatory agency isn't creating new restrictions, requirements, mandates and laws that make it increasingly more difficult to run your business and make a profit.

Business owners deserve better. They're responsible for generating the huge majority of the jobs in this country yet they seem too often to be treated like bad-guys. One of many problems business owners face today is the difficulty of obtaining credit and bank loans. Ever since the banking crisis, banks have over reacted and put a strangle-hold on lending. As you know, availability of funds is the lifeblood of any business yet it is still a big challenge with today's lending environment.

I'm sure at some time you've most likely had the experience of trying to obtain funding from a bank, right? This has got to be everyone's most hated experience. The banker starts out by requiring you to fill out an endless amount of forms. They survey your credit with an electron microscope and find things you've never imagined. You provide countless financial statements, tax returns, bank statements, reports, ledgers and endless requests for yet more information.

Then the bureaucratic hassles really begin. They finally send your loan package upstairs. Then it goes to the loan committee, then back and forth like a tennis match in a never- ending game of survivor. They might as well start off by telling you to get down on your hands and knees and beg and grovel. Then, to add insult to injury, if you're lucky, they come back and tell you they will loan you money up to the amount of collateral you put up.

There is a better way.

The Barefoot Retirement Plan is the best retirement plan you will find, and it's also an absolute God-Send to business owners. The humble little IUL program can be your answer to a ready source of capital that your business needs. And, the great part is, getting the funds is easy as pie.

Did you know that back in 1953 when Walt Disney was trying to start Disney Land, no bank would touch such a crazy idea? Lucky for Walt, he had a form of permanent life insurance that he was able to borrow against to make his dreams come true and change the world. J.C. Penny experienced a similar situation. He needed capital to keep his business going in the early days, and the banks would not step up. He was forced to turn to his life insurance policy to borrow the funds and without that, it's likely none of us would have ever heard of J.C. Penny.

Additionally, Ray Kroc, (McDonald's founder), and Doris Christopher (Pampered Chef founder) turned to their life insurance policies when no one else believed in them nor would lend them any money. Had it not been for their life insurance policies, we may have never heard of these businesses. These are just some of the most famous individuals to point to. There are countless other business owners who have relied on their life insurance policies to sustain them and help them to succeed.

We could devote an entire book to the many ways you can use this program in conjunction with your business but for the sake of brevity here, I will just point out the key benefits and usages of this program in your business.

The simplest way to look at it is; your IUL is the bank, and you're the owner of the bank. Imagine how great it would be to finally be able to fire your banker and put yourself in charge. Pretty good, right? You would be a one-man loan committee, and you get to approve all of your own loans. *Sweet!*

It really is as simple as this:

Step 1: Work with an experienced and knowledgeable IUL advisor that will take the time to evaluate your unique personal and business needs and structure the IUL that perfectly suits your needs. Set up one or more individual policies.

Step 2: Fund your IUL to the capital levels that work best for you.

Step 3: Allow the cash value of your account to build over time.

Step 4: When you need funds for your business or investment opportunities that come up, have a meeting with yourself and borrow the funds from your policy as needed.

Here is an example of how the meeting with yourself could go. You say to yourself, *"Self, I need to borrow some money from my IUL account for a great investment opportunity or to use in my business. Okay. Is it a good opportunity and does it make good business sense to do? Well yes. It is a great opportunity, and I have every confidence in the world that it will work out. Okay then. That's sounds good to me. I approve you being able to borrow the funds."*

That truly is about as hard as it is once you have the base of funds in your account. Not a bad meeting, right?

Let's look at a practical example of using the IUL in your business.

Let's say you own a machine shop, and you need a piece of equipment to expand and grow your business. You know you could generate more profits if you had that new piece of equipment.

You now know that you have two options for making this purchase.
(A new way of looking at it.)
Option A:

If you had the money, you could simply write a check and buy the machine. If you don't have the money, you can go back to your friendly banker and get back on your hands and knees.

However, with this program, you now have Option B.
Option B:

First set up and fund your IUL. (If you need the equipment right away, you can purchase a policy rider that will allow you to borrow the majority of the funds out within the first month.)

Then simply borrow the majority of the funds you put into your IUL and use those funds to buy the machine. All of the funds you put into the IUL are <u>NOW</u> working for you and earning between 0% to 17% tax-free per year (even though you borrowed against the policy), **AND** you also now have your new machine to expand and grow your business.

That's smart leverage.

If you use option A, you have your new piece of equipment, and that's it.

If you use option B, you have your new piece of equipment, **AND** you also now have a retirement fund or, in a sense, your own bank that you can continue to use going forward.

(Where I come from, we call this a "No-Brainer".)

It's like having your cake and eating it too.

We could review an endless number of scenarios with this. If you have a medical practice of any type, you most likely have an endless need for new equipment. Why not use this same method with all of your business needs?

Here is a short list of just some of the way's business owners can use this program.

- Financing business equipment, computer systems, tools, materials, office buildings, expansion, supplies, technology, etc.
- Financing your cars, trucks, business vehicles, planes, boats, etc.
- Funding a new business start-up, opening another practice, etc.

- Purchasing other companies, franchises, mergers, acquisitions, etc.

- Funding new key employee acquisition or employee expansion, etc.

- Offer IULs to partners and/or to attract and retain key employees

- Estate planning, partnership buy/sell agreements, etc.

- Fund a war-chest for the next economic downturn or unexpected emergency

- Use to bridge your receivables, tax bills

- Receive discounted prices for paying with cash

I'm sure you've already thought of other uses in your business for this amazing program. The value of having this option should not be underestimated. If/when we have another banking crisis again in this country and capital availability dries up, this could very well be your only predictable source of funds for a good period of time.

As you know, we've been in a low interest rate environment for quite a long time. As sure as the sun is going to come up tomorrow, you know that at some point, interest rates will rise again. The market is cyclical and the only thing we know for sure is that things will change. (I remember getting an 18.5% car loan back in the 1980s. *That was nuts.*)

How great would it be when that day does come, and rates are sky high, to have your own bank in place, in the form of your own IUL. Instead of having trot down to your local bank, get on your hands and knees and beg to pay them their exorbitant rates, you simply have another meeting with yourself.

You decide to borrow the funds from yourself, at much, much lower rates. Heck, if you want, you don't even have to pay the loan back, much less the interest (if structured correctly). How's that for a friendly banker? Just knowing that you have that flexibility and these options, is so liberating.

The Perfect Exit Strategy For Your Business

If you're like many business owners, at some point down the road, there's a good chance you would love to sell your business and enjoy the fruits of your labors. However, most business owners are so busy building their businesses that they've spent little time thinking about what they will actually do with the profits they receive when they sell it.

One thing you do know. You're going to have to pay a big chunk of your profits to Uncle Sam when you sell your business. So let's use an example. Let's say you sold your business, paid all the capital gains taxes on the proceeds of the sale, and are now left with a cool million dollars. What are you going to do with that money?

After you just gave all of that hard-earned money to Uncle Sam, there's a good chance that you're going to think about doing something with it that's taxed advantaged or tax exempt. You will want to keep as much of it as you can without giving your favorite uncle even more of your earnings. The problem is, there are no-good options out there for putting a lump sum of money like that into a tax-free program. So you are kind-of stuck here.

The good news is, there is a solution, if you plan ahead. Let's take a quick, high-level look at two different options. Let's say Bill is our business owner. His plan is to build his business for another 25 years, and then sell it and ride off into the sunset.

Option 1:

Bill talks with his financial advisor and decides to go with a qualified plan. Let's be generous and say he chooses a qualified plan that allows him to contribute up to $50,000 a year. The only problem is, in the early years, Bill's business needs cash. Lots of cash to keep things going. He would like to contribute the entire 50k per year, but he's only able to contribute $10,000 a year due to the cash demands of his business.

The problem is, qualified plans have a *Use-it-or-lose-it* provision. So in year 1, if Bill contributes $10,000 to his plan, the unused $40,000 of his contribution limit DOES NOT carry over to the next year. Not at all. You can clearly see how this strategy does not help Bill at all with his plan to preserve his profits when he sells his business.

Over the 25 years, Bill would have put $250,000 dollars into his qualified program. ($10,000 a year for 25 years.) He would have most likely invested them into equities and been subject to the up and down swings of the market place. Then, when he starts pulling the money out of his qualified plans, he will have to pay income taxes on every single penny he pulls out of the program. *All of it*. Can you even imagine what tax rates will be in 25 years?

Plus, after Bill sells his business, he still has to figure out what to do with his million-dollar net profit. In all likelihood, he will have to put it into a taxable investment and pay taxes on those funds again at some point. Sure seems like a rigged system doesn't it?

Option 2:

Bill talks with his Barefoot Retirement Plan advisor and decided to set up an IUL. One of the great features of an IUL is that, if it is set up correctly, it allows for very flexible premiums. (We will use a high-level, general example here to explain how this concept works.) Let's say Bill's IUL allowed for a maximum contribution per year of $50,000. However, Bill is still in the same cash position, so he can only contribute $10,000 a year to his IUL. That leaves an unused contribution amount of $40,000 a year.

Here is the BIG difference! The IUL allows Bill to CARRY OVER ANY UNUSED CONTRIBUTION AMOUNT. Here's the really cool part. It carries over *FOREVER*. It's true. So let's say Bill built his business for 25 more years and during each of those 25 years, he only contributed $10,000 a year to his IUL. He has 40k of unused contribution amounts for 25 years. $40,000 x 25 = $1,000,000 of missed premiums.

(Note, IUL policies vary from company to company. Some policies accommodate all the missed premiums, and others accommodate most, but not the full amount. If you are interested in a program like this, we will need to carefully and strategically plan for it in advance, so you will be able to take full advantage of it in the future.)

So now Bill can take the 1 million dollars he netted from the sale of his business and put it into his IUL to make up for the missed premiums. Wow! **That million dollars is now put into his policy and when he borrows against it to pull the money out, it will ALL be completely, 100% TAX-FREE!**

Now I ask you… where else can you do that? I'll tell you where. *No where!*

Plus, Bill put in the 10k a year for the 25 years. Over the 25 years, he would have earned between 0% and 17% per year (depending on the blended index performance) on those funds. He would have NEVER suffered a decline in value due to market performance. So he would have the value of these funds working for him in his IUL PLUS the 1 million dollars he just added to it. Plus, if he chose to, he could have borrowed funds from IUL at any time, and invested them into his business, or any other investment, to double dip on his returns.

There is not another option on the planet that will allow you to put large chunks of money into accounts where you can borrow all the money out tax-free like this. Can you imagine how much tax savings this strategy will save Bill? He's much better off. His family is much better off. It's a total win, win, win for Bill and his family. This just shows you the power that the IUL offers to business owners.

If you would like to see what this strategy would look like for you and your business, contact us, and we'll be happy to discuss this strategy with you and put together a custom plan that shows you how this can work for you.

To Schedule a Free, Private Consultation, Get Your Questions Answered And Have Custom illustrations Run For You:
Call Us : (866) 480-7784
Email Us: info@BarefootRetirement.com
Complete A Request Form At: www.BarefootRetirement.com/schedule

CHAPTER 21

The Best College Savings Program You've Never Heard Of

If you think this program looks good for adults structuring it for retirement, you should see how well it works for young children.

Talk about the perfect college savings fund, *this is it.*

Most of the traditional college type saving's funds out there are loaded with restrictions and limitations. As you know, this is different.

Most of the popular collage savings programs limit you and require that you ONLY use the funds for college tuition. If you take the funds out for any other reason, you get slapped with big penalties and/or fines. What if your child decides that college is not right for them? What if an unexpected emergency comes up, and you need the funds for something else? If you are stuck in one of those college savings programs, you simply do not have many good options. You either use the funds for college, or you are forced to pay the penalties and fees.

A properly structured and funded IUL can serve double duty. You can set it up to take care of your child's college expenses AND also serve as a retirement program for them.

Simply put, this is how it works.

You fund an IUL for your child. You can start at any age, even newborns. When your child reaches college age, IF they decide they don't want to go to college, no problem. YOU are in control. It's YOUR policy. You can use the funds for ANYTHING you want like helping your child start their own business, travel the world or covering medical expenses. You can spend the funds on *anything* wish; it doesn't matter. There are NO RESTRICTIONS on taking funds out and there are no penalties for taking funds out.

If your child does decide to go to college, you simply take loans out against the policy to pay for college. The funds in the policy

CONTINE to have the ability to grow, depending on market conditions, even though you borrowed against them.

You can then choose to pay back the loans, <u>or not</u>. Then you simply let the policy grow until your child reaches retirement and bingo, your child has a retirement program that they can rely on. This program quite simply beats the pants off of ANY other college saving program anywhere!

Check out how it compares to other plans on the chart below.

College Savings Programs – Options/Benefits	529 Plans	Student & Parent Loans	UGMAS & UTMAS	IUL
Unlimited amount of funds can be put into the program?	X	✓	✓	✓
Funds can be used for non-education purposes (Starting a business, medical, travel, retirement, etc.)	X	X	X	✓
Avoids having the funds count against you when applying for federal student aid	X	✓	X	✓
You have complete control over how and when the funds are used	X	X	X	✓
Plan has tax benefits	?	?	?	✓
Can never decrease in value due to market downturns	X	?	?	✓
Completely private program	X	X	X	✓
You can use the plan after college without owing any taxes	X	X	X	✓
Plan has option to borrow the funds and leverage them in other investment opportunities	X	X	X	✓

Just like for adults, we will be happy to run some analysis for you on your children, grandchildren, etc. When you factor in the years these young people will have to grow their IULs, the results can be amazing.

CHAPTER 22

Build a Retirement and Leave a Legacy

Most people's first goal is to take care of their own retirement needs. After all, who wants to spend their retirement years working all the time or simply eking out an existence? We only have one life to live, and I believe it should be lived to its fullest and lived with gusto! It's pretty hard to live your life to its fullest if you are broke or struggling to get by.

That's why we believe it's so important that you seriously consider the Barefoot Retirement Plan as a way to take care of your retirement needs so you can live that dream retirement.

Even if you started late or were not able to fund your IUL to the amount you wanted, and your lifetime annual funds that you borrow from your policy during retirement are somewhat modest, many people are shocked at how large their death benefit is with an IUL.

Hopefully at some point, you'll be in a position where your financial retirement needs are completely achieved. In a position where you're positive that even with a worst-case scenario, you will still have more than enough funds to live that retirement you've always dreamed about. Just imagine what a good feeling that's going to be!

For some, you will have more than enough retirement funds to take care of yourself and your spouse for as long as you may live. Once you reach that point, human nature naturally leads us to questions like this:

Did I make a difference? Did my life really matter? Did I leave my mark? Was my life significant? Did my life have meaning? Have I truly made a difference in the people's lives whom I touched in my life? How will I be remembered? Have I helped more people than have helped me? Are other's lives better because of me?

Here's one of my favorites by Nelson Henderson:

"The true meaning of life is to plant trees, under whose shade you do not expect to sit."

One of the great benefits of our program is that we can specifically design plans to help you leave a legacy. A legacy that will transcend your life and be a true blessing to your children, grandchildren, extended family, charities, businesses and much more. We can tailor these custom plans to help you protect, grow, and leverage your retirement savings so you will be able to leave a legacy that will positively impact others.

We know the importance of keeping complete control of your money while you are living. We also know that most people want to keep as much of their wealth as possible *in the family*. If you don't plan carefully, and correctly it's easy to watch your funds evaporate by going to nursing homes, hospitals, the IRS, unintended people or any of the many traps that can siphon off your wealth during the transfer to the next generation.

If you would like to leave a portion of your estate to charities, we can help you structure this so your complete needs and desires are taken care of first. Then the amount of funding you designated to go to charities will live on, benefiting others. What a true blessing that could be. You could make such a meaningful difference in the lives of others whom you will never know.

As you have learned, due to the many benefits of our program and the IUL, you have the potential to leave a much larger legacy than you otherwise could. Many clients are shocked at just how large they are able to grow their accounts with this amazing program.

I think there are a handful of people who when they pass away, plan to leave their estate to the Government. Ha. The huge majority of people already leave far too much to the Government as it is in the form of taxes, estate taxes, death taxes and the like.

If you feel like you've already given the Government *your fair share*, you will be delighted to know that all of your IUL funds are completely tax-free. Thus, it's likely that you'll be able to leave much more to charity or to your family than you had thought. With just about any other program out there, you would have had to pay a very hefty percentage of your funds to the Government. With our IUL program, a 100% of your funds are free from all taxes.

We know how to navigate the waters of estate planning. Utilizing techniques to lock in current estate values, gift exemptions, and design plans to utilize all of your annual gift exemptions so you don't waste any of your available tax savings. If we went in to all the methods and strategies we use, we would overflow the pages in this book! Just be assured that if you are concerned with the challenge of transferring your wealth to the next generation, charities, etc., we have the creative solutions to you need to ensure that your legacy is left intact, and as you wanted it.

We sincerely hope that we can help to make a positive difference in your life. It would be an honor for us to help you structure a plan that helps you achieve your goals and hopefully leave a legacy that will be such a blessing to others.

CHAPTER 23

Frequently Asked Questions

Below is a list of some of the questions that are asked most frequently by our clients.

Q. Can I own more than one IUL policy?

A. Yes. Any individual can own multiple different IUL policies. And, each policy can have a different owner, insured and beneficiary. A family could have a policy for each spouse and one for each of the children, grandchildren, etc. Plus you can set up policies for your businesses as well.

Q. I'm stuck in a bad insurance policy. Can I switch over to an IUL?

A. Yes. You can easily use a 1035 exchange to do this. It allows you to move your money from your poorly performing policy to another better performing policy, while keeping your tax basis the same.

Q. Most of my retirement funds are tied up in my IRA and 401(k). Can I switch them from those programs, to and IUL?

A. Yes. It is important to keep in mind that there are different tax ramifications depending on your age and income. It's always best to consult your tax and securities advisor prior to liquidating any qualified funds. We do have clients who are so frustrated with the performance of their current retirement programs that they are willing to take the tax hit now, to be able to sleep better at night.

Q. Can I really miss or skip premium payments and still keep my policy intact?

A. Yes. This is a BIG benefit to the IUL. When you have a properly structured policy, you have almost infinite flexibility with your annual contribution amounts. When we design your custom plan, we do analysis to determine the appropriate death benefit amount. The death benefit has two important minimum and maximum numbers. In between those numbers is the flexibility you have.

There is a minimum amount you can contribute per year. This is what the insurance company defines as the minimum amount needed to pay for their cost to insure you. The maximum amount is defined by the IRS, and it's based on the amount of death benefit attached to your plan. We're happy to run some analysis for you to show you what your numbers look like.

Life is full of surprises and changes, so it's comforting to know that you have *tremendous flexibility* with your IUL contributions, without having to worry about negative effects to your policy.

Often, just the first few months of contributions is WELL over the minimum annual amount necessary to keep your plan active.

This premium flexibility is something our clients really appreciate. Other plans require set premiums, and if they aren't paid, it can have VERY negative effects on the policy's performance.

Q. How safe is my money in an IUL policy?

A. As discussed earlier, we work with the highest rated Mutual Insurance companies. Most of these companies have been in business over 100 years. They have withstood the test of time, and survived and thrived. In today's crazy financial markets, we believe these companies are among the safest companies in the world. Plus, since they are mutual companies, and not publicly owned stock companies, they are not as subject to much of the madness of Wall Street.

Q. What are the downsides to an IUL?

A. The IUL has the same downsides and risks that are associated with any retirement plan, but on a much smaller scale due to the floors, caps, and other protections that are in place. When you understand the benefits of an IUL, you'll find that almost all the "downsides" are associated with short-term pain to receive long-term gain. IE: Short Term 'cost of insurance' expense, to receive long-term, tax-free income, and death benefit.

Q. Can Canadians use this same Barefoot Retirement Plan, eh?

A. Yes. Not all of the Insurance providers we work, offer policies that will work in Canada, but we do have some great providers that will.

Q. **How does an IUL compare overall to an IRA, 401(k) and ROTH account?**

A. Good question. We thought the easiest way to show this would be in the chart below. We simply took the most important, key factors of retirement plans, and compared them all together. We think the chart speaks for itself.

Program Features and Benefits	Qualified Plans (IRA/401k)	ROTH	IUL
Has No Market Risk (If savings are based on market returns)	X	X	✓
Has Life Insurance Included	X	X	✓
Has No Contribution Limit	X	X	✓
Funds Can Be Accessed Tax Free	X	✓	✓
Is Private	X	X	✓
Has Investment Restrictions or Prohibited Transactions	X	X	✓
Can Borrow Your Funds With No Repayment Required	X	X	✓
Loans Can Be Used For Anything	X	X	✓
Use For "Be Your Own Banker" Concept	X	X	✓
Earnings Can Be Accessed Before Age 59 ½ With No IRS Penalty	X	X	✓
Required Minimum Distribution Not Required at Age 70 ½	X	✓	✓
Income Not Included In Formula To Tax Social Security	X	✓	✓
Remainder Left To Heirs Income Tax-Free	X	✓	✓

Chapter 24

What We Know and What We Don't Know

There are no guarantees in life.

You know that.

Some aspects of our IUL program ARE contractually guaranteed. However, no one knows how the market indexes will perform over the next few decades. No one knows what will happen with the US, and world economy in the future.

But Here Are a Few Things We Do Know.

We know the insurance company we most often use for our type of IUL is one of the strongest companies in the world. They've withstood the test of time for over 130 years and have always succeeded in spite of facing the biggest challenges this world has ever seen.

We know that over the last 24 years, the blended market index we use has averaged a 9.28% return. Anything could change in the future, but that's not too bad for a 24 year track record.

We know the IUL account will NEVER lose money due to market downturns. Regardless of what happens, your gains are always locked in, because of the zero % floor that's set in place.

We know that if you structure, fund and manage your policy properly, with our guidance, the funds you borrow out to live on during your retirement years will be 100% completely tax-free. We don't know where tax rates will go in the future, but it doesn't really matter to us, since we know we won't have to worry about it.

We know in most cases, depending on the state laws where you live, your retirement funds will be safe and secure from creditors, and from lawsuits, bankruptcies, etc. We know we live in a litigious society, and that these days you can get sued for practically anything. It's great to know that your retirement funds are safe and protected.

We know that if you structure, fund and manage your policy correctly, you have the contractual ability to be provided with a tax-free retirement income for as long as you live. A tax-free, guaranteed income for life. Boy, doesn't that sound good.

We know you can access your money at any time you wish. You can pull out any amount of money that you wish, for any reason. There are no restrictions or requirements. It's great to know that if a medical, business, or personal emergency comes up; you have a ready resource of cash that you can turn to any time you want.

We know that your account, its value, and its earnings, are completely PRIVATE. There is NO Government reporting required at all. As our lives are becoming less private by the day, this is very comforting to know.

WE CHALLENGE YOU

Is the Barefoot Retirement Plan perfect? Nope. Nothing is.

You don't just set up an IUL and boom; all of your financial concerns are instantly solved. It does take some time for your account to build and grow. Over time is when the true magic happens.

However, we will go on record to say that we believe this is THE finest, and most beneficial retirement program ever created, PERIOD.

The Barefoot Retirement management team has decades of experience in this industry. We've never seen anything come close to being as good as this program is.

The most common reaction we get from potential clients when they see this is; first, their jaw drops to the floor and then they say, *"Wow, I've never seen anything even half as good as this, ever."*

If they don't respond like that, they typically fall into the group that feels it's *"Too good to be true," "Nothing is that good," "If this is true, I would have heard about this before,"* etc., etc.

It's easy to see how a program this amazing, could be hard to believe that it's as good as it is. That's why we encourage you to look into this further and see what you're on Barefoot Retirement could look like.

CHAPTER 25

How To Get Started

Want To See How YOUR Barefoot Retirement Could Look?

We would love to schedule a completely free phone consultation with one of our specialty trained retirement experts. They will take a few minutes on the phone and discuss your specific situation, your needs, your goals and what you would like to accomplish. Any questions you have, we'll be happy to answer them. After we gather some key points of information, we will run an illustration for you, (or several different illustrations if you wish), that will show you in detail exactly what your retirement could look like with an IUL that meets your needs.

If you don't have a large amount of funds to invest into an IUL, it's okay. Typically, all you need to get started is about $300 a month or so. Plus, our agents can usually help you easily discover ways and sources of funds that would be perfect for your IUL that most people never think of. After all, when something is this good, most people want to put as much into it as they can.

If you're a large investor and have millions of dollars to invest, we work with clients such as yourself all the time. In fact, we specialize in high net-worth clients. We can help you develop brilliantly customized solutions for your business, key employees, family, etc. that will beat the pants off of anything else you've ever seen.

In fact, as I am writing this book, we are working with a client and structuring a plan for him to put a million dollars a year into an IUL for himself. Then he wants to set up IULs for his spouse, and his children. After that, he wants to work on setting up IULs for his key employees. He is even looking into switching from his company's current 401(k) plan, to an IUL plan for all of his employees.

We are happy to confidentially discuss this program with you, and answer all of your questions. We will run custom illustrations, and review them in detail with you, all completely free of charge. No obligation whatsoever.

Our Approach

We know your retirement is serious business. We know this is something that takes some time to understand and absorb. You will find our approach to be that of a helpful consultant, providing you with the information you need.

We're here to work with the clients who have an interest in this program, and help them structure a customized program that best meets their unique goals, needs and desires. You won't find any traditional *"pushy salesmen"* with our firm. We don't tolerate them.

We think you'll find our approach to be a *"breath of fresh air"* compared to what you may have experienced in the past.

To request your free analysis you can either give us a call at: **866-480-7784**

Or complete a request form at: www.BarefootRetirement.com/schedule

Or send us an email at: info@BarefootRetirement.com

Or you can complete the request form at the back of this book, and mail it in to us, or fax it to us.

To Schedule a Free, Private Consultation, Get Your Questions Answered And Have Custom illustrations Run For You:
Call Us : (866) 480-7784
Email Us: info@BarefootRetirement.com
Complete A Request Form At: www.BarefootRetirement.com/schedule

We look forward to hearing from you and helping you any way we can.

By the way, a lot of our clients feel like kicking themselves because they did not find out about this sooner. There's hardly a day that goes by that we don't hear someone saying, *"Man, I wish I had started this program 20 years ago."*

We totally know how you feel. However, consider this wise ancient Chinese proverb:

*"The Best Time To Plant a Tree Was 20 Years Ago.
The Second Best Time Is Now."*

Chapter 26

Two Paths to Choose From

All of us have options. Now that you've seen the Barefoot Retirement Program, you realize you don't have to keep your retirement constrained by all of the traditional limitations of qualified retirement accounts. *You now know there's a better way.* A MUCH better way!

The *easy* thing to do (for now), is to do nothing. Just continue doing what you've been doing and hoping it will yield better results down the road.

However, I challenge you to carefully consider this program. **DO IT NOW** while you still have time to do something about it. After all, the longer you wait, the more limited your options will become and the less time you'll have for this amazing program to perform. Don't be the guy who looks back one day and says, *"I shouldda, couldda, wouldda."*

Mark Twain once said, *"Twenty years from now you will be more disappointed by the things you did not do, than by the things you did do."*

What If…

What if the market takes a huge nose dive right before you get ready to retire, and your retirement account drops like a rock?

What if tax rates are double what they are now when you retire? It could be devastating.

This program allows you to LOCK IN these important benefits, so you don't have to risk it.

Why take the chance, if you don't have to?

After all, what could be more important than insuring that you have planned wisely, and are well taken care of in your retirement?

Trust me. You will have a lot of time to think about this when you retire. Make sure those are good thoughts, about the wise decisions you made prior to retirement.

Thanks for taking your valuable time to read this book. We sincerely hope you found it as eye-opening and helpful as most people do when they discover these amazing concepts.

I wish you the very best life has to offer.

Whatever your vision is for your own barefoot retirement; I hope you get to live it.

God Bless.

CHAPTER 27

For Insurance Professionals

If you're an insurance professional and would like to explore how you can gain access to our patented version of the IUL and use it to help your clients achieve their retirement goals, give us a call.

We are selective and only work with agents to put their client's needs, above their own. It's most important to us that we have similar philosophies and mindsets on this.

We contract with hundreds of agents and large numbers of agencies to offer this unique program. There's hardly a day that goes by when we don't talk with a very successful agency that exclusively deals with high-end professionals.

Most of them thought they had heard and *seen it all*. They know of all the products and programs that are available in the marketplace. Often, they have the same response that many of our clients do… *"Wow; I've never seen anything as powerful as this! This is amazing. How can we offer this?"*

If you think you may be a good fit for our approach and what we offer, give us a call. We would love to speak with you.

We look forward to hearing from you.

CHAPTER 28

Your Free, No-Obligation Analysis Request Form

☐ *Yes!* I want to see what my Barefoot Retirement would look like. Please have a Barefoot Retirement advisor contact me and put together a completely free, no-obligation retirement analysis for me. I understand that you never use high-pressure tactics, and I will not be asked to purchase anything during this meeting. It is a consultative meeting, not a sales meeting. (Please print very clearly and use black ink.)

Name: _____

Address: _____

City: _____ State: _____ Zip: _____

Day Phone: _____ Evening Phone: _____

Primary Email Address: _____

What is the best time to speak with you during business hours?

_____

Please know that we will NEVER sell, rent, trade, barter, or use your information in any way, ever. It will be kept completely confidential. We will only use this information to aid your advisor in preparing your analysis. By completing this information you authorize Barefoot Retirement to contact you to create your free analysis.

Please tell us a little about yourself, so we can use the time we spend with you most effectively. This information will remain completely private.

	You	**Your spouse or significant other**
Age:	_____	_____
Occupation:	_____	_____
Annual Income:	_____	_____
Age you would like to retire:	_____	_____
Do you own your home(s)?	_____	
Approximate mortgage balance:	_____	
Do you own your own business(s)?	_____	
If yes, what type(s):	_____	
Your biggest concern about retirement?	_____	
You biggest financial concern?	_____	
How did you hear about us?	_____	

Thanks for completing this information.

Option 1: Fax this form to us at: **215-623-1139**

Option 2: Mail this form to us at:

Barefoot Retirement, 402A W. Palm Valley Blvd., #237 Round Rock, Texas 78664

CHAPTER 29

General Disclaimer

A great deal of care, effort and attention has been taken to provide current and accurate information regarding the subject matter covered in this book. Neither the author, Doyle Shuler, nor the publisher is responsible for any errors or omissions, or for the results obtained from the use of the information in this book. The information contained in this book is intended to provide general information, and does not constitute financial, legal, tax, or investment advice, and may not be relied upon for purposes of avoiding any Federal or State taxes or penalties. Neither the information presented in this book nor any opinions expressed, constitutes a representation by us or a solicitation of the purchase or sale of any securities.

All the information and content of this book are provided "as is," and there are no guarantees of completeness, accuracy, and/or timeliness of information. This information is not intended to cover all aspects of a particular matter. Doyle Shuler is not a licensed insurance agent. This book is written for educational purposes. There is no guarantee of successful results by using the information contained within this book. We do not control the markets, nor the economy, nor can we control what you do nor how and when you do it. There is no warranty associated with this book, neither expressed nor implied including but not limited to warranties of merchantability, performance, suitableness or fitness for any particular purpose. Your use of the information contained within this book is at your own risk. You assume full and complete responsibility and all risk of loss that may result from the use of information contained here. Neither Doyle Shuler, Smart Retire Plan, LLC, Multiple Streams Marketing, LLC, Barefoot Retirement, Dove Ventures, partners, agents, employees, providers, nor related corporations and partnerships, nor any advisors or investment providers will be liable for any direct, indirect, incidental, special, consequential, inadvertent or punitive damages or any damages what so ever, whether in an action based upon a statute, contract, tort, including but not limited to negligence or otherwise, relating to the use and application of this information. In no event will Doyle Shuler, Smart Retire Plan, LLC, Multiple Streams Marketing, LLC, Barefoot Retirement, Dove Ventures, nor related corporations and partnerships, nor any advisors or investment providers nor partners, agents, employees, or providers thereof be liable in any way to the reader nor any other person, company, organization or entity for any actions, investments or decisions taken on the reliance of the information contained in this book, and/or related websites, videos, links, references, financial calculators, the Barefoot Retirement calculator, publications, emails, resources and/or associates for any consequential, unique, special, similar, unintended damages, even if advised of the possibility of such damages. Doyle Shuler, Smart Retire Plan, LLC, Multiple Streams Marketing, LLC, Barefoot Retirement, Dove Ventures, nor related corporations and partnerships, nor any advisors or investment providers nor partners, agents, employees, or providers are engaged in rendering any legal, accounting, investment, tax, psychological, or professional services. You should always seek the services of a competent professional for advice regarding legal, accounting, investment, tax, psychological, or professional services. It is important to remember that individual situations can and do vary, thus not all information is applicable to all people. It is acknowledged that even though the information contained within this book was thought to be correct and accurate at the time this book was published; it is very likely that it has or may become outdated and obsolete by changes in the law, Government, tax structure, the economy, the industry, the marketplace, rates, percentages, assumptions, returns, and changes in general. Thus, the facts, figures, rates, returns, examples, assumptions, and the like are not guaranteed and are completely subject to change. If there have been any degrading, limiting, or doubtful slights made against any products, companies, plans, programs, investments, individuals, institutions, organizations, systems or otherwise, are unintentional. Per examples and stories, testimonials and the like used in the book, individual and institutional results can and do vary based on a range of variable factors that are unique to each individuals, families, companies, and organizations situation. All retirement and investment plans and programs contain risk. It is possible that you can lose some or all of your funds if you deploy them according to the methods outlined in this book or any other methods used.

The End

www.ingramcontent.com/pod-product-compliance
Lightning Source LLC
Chambersburg PA
CBHW071424170526
45165CB00001B/391